TENTH EDITION *Update*

THE R110
STUDENT COURSEBOOK

to accompany

THE ART *of* PUBLIC SPEAKING

NINTH EDITION • STEPHEN E. LUCAS

Written and Compiled by

Jennifer Cochrane
Kate Thedwall
Kathy F. Vancil

Department of Communication Studies
IU School of Liberal Arts at
Indiana University Purdue University Indianapolis

This book contains material for
R110, THE FUNDAMENTALS OF SPEECH COMMUNICATION
for IUPUI and IUPU—Columbus Classes

Learning Solutions

Boston   Burr Ridge, IL   Dubuque, IA   New York   San Francisco   St. Louis
Bangkok   Bogotá   Caracas   Lisbon   London   Madrid
Mexico City   Milan   New Delhi   Seoul   Singapore   Sydney   Taipei   Toronto

The R110 Student Coursebook
to accompany
The Art of Public Speaking, Ninth Edition

2 3 4 5 6 7 8 9 0 QPD QPD 0 9 8

ISBN-13: 978-0-07-353822-8
ISBN-10: 0-07-353822-1

Editor: Ann Hayes
Production Editor: Kathy Phelan
Cover Photos: WOMAN WITH MICROPHONE: The McGraw-Hill Companies, Inc./Gary He, photographer; SPEAKING IN SCRUBS: The McGraw-Hill Companies, Inc./Andrew Resek, photographer; GRADUATION: Comstock Images / JupiterImages; SENATOR JOHN EDWARDS: Kerry-Edwards 2004, Inc./Dave Scull, photographer; HAND GESTURES: The McGraw-Hill Companies, Inc./Andy Resek, photographer
Printer/Binder: Quebecor World

CONTENTS

ACKNOWLEDGMENTS

Aha! So you are not the average student who considers "acknowledgments" a list of boring "thank yous!" Read on and you may find out some interesting stuff about this course.

R110, *The Fundamentals of Public Speaking,* was made possible by years and years of sweat and toil on the parts of Drs. David Burns and B. Bruce Wagener. These two innovators built the course, wrote a textbook and invented the Speech Night Contest. Dr. Wagener, who retired in June of 1998, "willed" the course to IUPUI-R110 faculty to update. Dr. Dorothy Webb, former Chair of the Department of Communication Studies, supported this endeavor by creating an advisory task force for the purpose of redesigning R110. Without the support and encouragement of these people, this course would not exist in its present form.

This advisory task force was composed of some teachers you may know: Ken Ayers, Mike Ayers, Jennifer Cochrane, Steve Comiskey, Dr. Catherine Dobris, Kathy Fox, Ron Sandwina, Cheryl Saugstad, Tom Stuckey, Kate Thedwall and Dr. Dorothy Webb. These people worked long hours to have a textbook adopted and a custom publisher selected in time for you to read *The Art of Public Speaking* by Stephen E. Lucas and use this custom coursebook by Fall semester 1998.

Vancil, Thedwall, and Cochrane wrote and will continue to modify the coursebook with continual feedback from R110 faculty and students. The initial version of the coursebook was done over a 3-month period and was not an easy project. Steve Comiskey and Moffett Craig were responsible for the Departmental "exit" or "final" exam. Once again, it was not a simple thing. Larry Cistrelli contributed his assignment for Outside Speaker Report #2. Eric Bruce was the creative mind behind the electronic portion of the Speech To Explain. Assisting with grading policies and giving excellent feedback to the project were members of the R110 faculty: Janis Crawford, Marsha Grant, Jay Newlin, Sally Nichols, Cheryl Saugstad, Gale Sturm, Dr. Robert Dick and Wayne Olson. We even had Kate Thedwall's R110 students, Erica Tupper, Mary Jane George, Jeff Miller and Bonnie Brock, evaluate our textbook possibilities! Also, thanks go to Dr. B. Bruce Wagener for inventing the One-Point Persuasive Speech and giving us permission to use it.

We are exceedingly grateful to Kim Rackliffe, our McGraw-Hill representative, who led us through a maze of teaching materials, and to Jan Scipio, our first custom publishing editor who helped us get this coursebook on paper. These ladies were always there when we needed them. We are also indebted to Amy Jones, our current McGraw-Hill representative; Don Reynolds, Regional Manager; and Tammy Immell, editor; for their encouragement and support.

We are startled and amazed and grateful to the scads of people who did not say "NO" when we came to them with our visions for this course. For example, librarians Bill Orme and Steve Schmidt, IUPUI and Janet Feldmann, IUPU Columbus, took it upon themselves to contribute information which would help us all negotiate the "information highway." Dr. Garland Elmore, David Donaldson, Bill Cuttrill, Dave Zaiser and Dennis Henderson who said NO PROBLEM when we asked them if we could tape about 5000 speeches this semester. Dr. Bill Taylor, IUPUI, and Dr. Bill Roberson, IUPU Columbus, said NO PROBLEM when we asked them to find equipment to tape all IUPUI off-campus students and all students at IUPU Columbus.

We are pleased to acknowledge and thank Dr. Ulla Connor, Susan Schumacher, Patrick Nolan and Dr. Giles Hoyt for providing tremendous insights into our strategies for mainstreaming the ESL student.

More thanks are due to Mike Maitzen, Mike Scott, Michelle Simmons, Cam Hopson and staff of the MLRC who saved us countless hours by helping us with any electronic problem we had during the whole project. Kudos go to the staff of the Center For Teaching and Learning for helping us get this book onto two different computer platforms.

During the 2005 academic year, R110 faculty reviewed, edited and reworked all of the speaking assignments. They graciously offered sample speeches, outlines, analyses, and self-evaluations for your use. The R110 faculty members are: Angela Apple, Larry Cistrelli, Steve Comiskey, Greg Cook, Moffett Craig, Jan DeWester, Dina David, Harold Donle, Donna Edmond, Omar Habayeb, Mariah Hayes, Sumana Jogi, Andrew Kerr, Steve LeBeau, Krista Longtin, Jennifer Medcalfe, Maureen Minielli, Sanda Neubauer, Kate Nicholson, Wayne Olson, Sally Perkins, Mike Polites, Paul Porter, Jack Price, Charles Reyes, Tom Stuckey, and Teresa Tackett.

If you've bothered to read this far, you may have concluded that this course has been reconfigured by the people who teach it and supported by many other departments and areas of the university. This is not a normal thing that happens in academic circles. It was a group effort and we are grateful for the "gift" of this project and even more grateful for all the people who were and are so willing to contribute their time, their talents and even their prayers for this course. Thanks, thanks, thanks to everyone.

Although this acknowledgment is last on paper, it should be first. We would like to thank God for bringing us to and through this project. He was there directing our path and guiding us every step of the way. ***Thank you, God!***

ACADEMIC SUPPORT

A MESSAGE TO THE STUDENT

It is not abnormal to hear any student say, "I don't understand why we are required to DO this! It doesn't seem relevant!" In *The Fundamentals of Public Speaking* (R110), we hear these sentiments expressed more frequently than we'd like.

We want to take this opportunity to explain the foundations upon which this course was created with the hope that you will better understand some of the assignments that are required of you. At the outset, this explanation may fit into your personal "boring" category; however, you may want to come back to it as you make your way through the course. These explanations may help you to justify, even appreciate your assignments as true opportunities for real learning!

As formulated by the R110 Task Force, here are the ten learning objectives upon which all your assignments, both oral and written, are based:

A student should be able to . . .

1. Learn how to listen (ethically and effectively).
2. Understand the importance of audience analysis and to be able to conduct worthwhile audience analyses and apply the result.
3. Master different systems of organization and apply appropriate organization to different types of speeches.
4. Develop and exhibit critical thinking and logical reasoning.
5. Improve (achieve) clarity of oral and written ideas.
6. Learn and use appropriate principles of persuasion in speaking assignments.
7. Practice appropriate delivery skills.
8. Use credible research tools.
9. Incorporate technology appropriate to speech making.
10. Fairly and constructively evaluate his/her speeches and those of others.

Reading through these, you may have found yourself wishing that if you only had to order a couple of items from the above menu, that would be enough! However, if you are to achieve any degree of effectiveness in public speaking, you have to "taste" a little of each of the above. **Now here they are again, in some detail:**

1. **How to be a good listener?** Well, it takes a while to learn, but there are several ways we propose to get you started. First, good listening is crucial to your success in this course or any course. The

Listening Sheets which accompany each assignment will help you to focus your listening by asking you to listen for certain aspects of your classmates' speeches. This will be very hard at first, but you will get better at it as you practice. **Your text** has a very practical chapter on listening with some great techniques suggested to improve your skill. You also will be asked to orally evaluate your classmates when they speak. For this, responsible listening on your part is crucial. (Read Lucas, Chapter 3)

2. Did you know that you have to understand **the physical and intellectual make-up of your audience** before you can effectively communicate with them? You will hear the words "Audience Analysis/Adaptation" over and over. **Chapter 5** in your text is very strong in this area. You will be asked to consider your audience makeup during every speech by preparing the **"Audience Analysis/Adaptation Sheet"** and handing it in before your speech. On this sheet you will be asked to discover a different aspect of your audience and use this information to make your speech more relevant for them.

3. Everyone has thoughts and ideas. Are you able to order them logically and clearly so that the majority of people can understand them? This logical sequencing of facts and ideas is called "organization" and you will be asked to **arrange your ideas or those of others in a pattern appropriate to the type of speech** you are assigned. This pattern is called an **"outline"** and is required for every speech. Basically it is like a blueprint for your thoughts, or like an itinerary for a trip, complete with road signs! It helps you to get where you are going and hopefully your audience will be following right along with you. (**Chapters 8 & 10** will help you here.)

4. **"A critical thinker and a logical reasoner."** Does this phrase describe you? If not, how soon would you like to get started? Your text addresses critical thinking in **Chapter 1.** A related subject, **"Guidelines for Ethical Listening" can be found in Chapter 2.** This segment is preceded by an entire chapter on ethical speaking. Chapters 15 and 16 are introductions to the art of persuasion which involves critical thinking as well as logical reasoning. You will be asked in the **Listening Sheets,** and the **Audience Analysis/Adaptation Sheets** and in your **Self-Evaluation Sheet** to think critically about and respond to any number of aspects of public speaking. You will be practicing the art of critically **discerning credible sources** of information for your speeches. You will be asked to **use this information logically in your persuasive arguments.**

5. **How clearly do you state your thoughts and ideas?** Is your language and syntax clear and descriptive enough that your audience can "see," "repeat," "feel," what you are saying? You will be getting plenty of **practice in speaking assignments and in oral peer evaluations** in class. Your **personal rehearsal** sessions will be time to practice language clarity. Practice-practice-practice. **Listen carefully to your evaluations. Read Chapter 11 on language!**

6. Are you aware of how often in a day you are required to **"persuade"** people or change their minds so that they believe, feel, or act differently? Did you know that good persuasion follows certain principles? **Chapters 15 & 16** in your text explain these principles and you will be given **two opportunities to give persuasive speeches.** Your **Listening Sheets** focus your listening on these principles as they are revealed (or not) in the speeches of your classmates. Your **Audience Analysis/Adaptation Sheets** require you to take your audience's feelings, beliefs and attitudes into consideration as you prepare your persuasive arguments.

7. Have you ever heard someone say, "It's not **what** you said, it's **how** you said it!"? Although it's not the major focal point in this course, delivery **is** crucial. Just by altering the mechanics of your voice you can change completely the meanings of your words, convey attitude, express feeling. Your

delivery is the *way* you express your thoughts, beliefs and ideas. Is your delivery appropriate? **Your instructor will take time (orally and in writing) after every speech** to tell you how you can improve in this area. **Listen up!** Your "delivery" even extends to times when you are not giving speeches; you are being judged during those times as well. **Chapter 12** is full of well-grounded tips on delivering speeches.

8. **Do you repeat everything you hear as truth? Do you include any fact or idea from anywhere or anyone in your term paper?** Do you believe all that is written in the *National Enquirer?* How about the *Wall Street Journal* or the Proctor and Gamble Web site? For all speeches except the Speech of Introduction, you will required to do some kind of formal research and in every assignment a certain number of sources are required. **Chapter 6** introduces you to research and gives you criteria for judging source reliability. You will be asked to **cite** these sources orally and in written form in each speech as well as **provide a works cited** at the end of your written outline.

9. How, you may ask, **is technology appropriate to speech making? Assignment #3, the Speech to Explain,** is an informative speech where you will be given the **opportunity to do research from library databases and internet sources.** Maybe you've already done this kind of research for another class. Anyone can put anything on the Internet. How do you know what's true and what's not? Again, **Chapter 6** gives you criteria for discerning credible (believable) Internet sources. Also, you are **required in Speech #3 to generate two professional-looking visuals** from PowerPoint or similar software. These skills will have many advantages beyond this class.

10. Finally, what makes an effective speech? Would you be able to **constructively evaluate the speeches of your classmates, your own speeches, or the speeches of others?** You will be using those **Listening Sheets for your peers.** You'll be given a chance to **evaluate orally,** like we've mentioned. You will be able to write an insightful **self-evaluation each time you speak** by reviewing your speeches on videotape (each of your speeches will be taped.) But what about speeches outside the classroom? Your instructor will give you an opportunity to write **an analysis of a live speech or a videotape-recorded one.** You'll be able to test your newly-developed insights in public speaking in one of these two situations.

If you got this far in your reading you can see that you have the opportunity to learn a great deal. Keep in mind that you can't learn everything in 16 weeks, but you surely can get a good start. The next portions of this coursebook provide much of what you need to know to make your experience in public speaking a success. Read them carefully and thoroughly.

This Coursebook has been put together for the IUPUI and IUPU Columbus campuses jointly. There are parts of this book that are appropriate to one campus or the other. We hope these are marked clearly and that you are not confused. On the other hand, if you have suggestions for improvement, please put them on paper and hand them to your instructor to give to the authors of this book. We will be more than happy to consider your ideas for the next edition.

Sincerely,

Jennifer Cochrane
Kate Thedwall
Kathy Fox Vancil

How to use This Book to Learn More and get a Better Grade in This Course!

- If you read and use this book systematically, it will increase your chances of accomplishing the course objectives of R110.

- The Coursebook is divided into four major parts: Academic Support, Policies and Procedures, The Preparation Outline, and the Speaking Assignments. Everything you need to know about the course, speech preparation, and grading is covered in this book.

- Of particular note is the Speaking Assignments section, which tells you what, why, and how to prepare your speeches.

- If you have a question about what to do for your speech, **look in this book first.**

- The Speaking Assignment section is divided into sections that contain info about each assignment. Your teacher will tell you which 5 speeches you are supposed to give.

- Once you know which assignment to work on, do this:

  - Read the unit description, then read the rationale for the speech because it will tell you why you need to learn how to give a speech of this type.

  - Then read about the benefits, what the audience's response to this type of speech should be, and what skills you will learn.

  - Check out any sample topics listed and then read the speech requirements carefully.

  - Check out the SAMPLE outlines, audience analyses, and self-evaluations. **Although they aren't perfect, they are excellent examples of what you paperwork should look like.**

- EVERY REQUIREMENT TRANSLATES INTO OR HELPS YOU ACQUIRE A SPEECH-MAKING SKILL. This course has a lot of requirements for each assignment. **There is a reason for every requirement.** If you are not sure what it is, please ask your instructor immediately.

- The **task checklist** is to help you organize your approach to the speech. You cannot prepare a speech the night before you give it and expect to fulfill the requirements in a satisfactory way.

- Look at the grading criteria on the speaker outline evaluation forms. **So many students lose points because they don't fulfill the speaking or the outlining criteria.** Make sure you have everything required or you will lose points! If you are not sure about the requirement or you did not talk about it in class, ask your instructor before you give your speech.

A Message to the ESL Student

If you are a student who speaks English as a second language, welcome to R110, **The Fundamentals of Speech Communication!** As you may know, we no longer offer a class only for ESL speakers. We felt that one of the best ways for you to learn our language is to be with native speakers. We are confident that you will learn better this way.

From our experience we know that ESL students have many of the same problems that all students have in public speaking classes such as nervousness, eye contact or the organization of a topic. At the same time we know that you may experience a few different problems than native speakers. This is quite normal and perfectly OK. Our faculty is very willing to help you, but you must ask for that help. Sometimes it is hard for your instructor to know you are having trouble if you do not tell him/her that you are having a problem. Also consider using the Speaker's Lab frequently for help with your difficulties or concerns.

We also are confident that you have a great deal to teach us as we work together.

Please do not hesitate to consult with your teacher as you take this class. Some of the things you will be asked to do may seem difficult or do not line up with your way of thinking. These difficulties may disappear, as you understand their cultural basis. So please, talk frequently with your instructor so that you have a successful experience in **The Fundamentals of Speech Communication.**

A WORD ABOUT ONCOURSE CL

Oncourse CL is the new online teaching and learning environment for the IU system. R110, The Fundamentals of Speech Communication, uses this environment to enhance your learning. You may be asked to submit homework via Oncourse CL Assignments, participate in a discussion using the CL Forums discussion tool, or communicate with your instructor by email (Messages) as a part of your R110 class. Here are some general tips for using Oncourse CL:

- You will need your network ID and password in order to log on to this environment. If you do not have either of these things, or you don't remember your password, go to the UITS Support Center in the IT building at IUPUI or through staff support at the IUPUC computer labs.

- Once you have your ID and password, go to this address on your computer: *<https://oncourse.iu.edu/>*

- Log in with your network ID and password and take a tour of this environment if you are not familiar with it. (See: Help at bottom of left hand navigation bar.)

- You also can get help with Oncourse CL at any of the university computer labs or consult the Oncourse Help tutorial at bottom of left-hand toolbar. **You may also ask for help at the Speaker's Lab**. UITS will offer classes to support student using Oncourse CL. See class schedules at *<http://ittraining.iu.edu>*

- Make sure you can locate the email tool (Messages) as well as the discussion forum (Forums) and grade book (Gradebook) in the left-hand toolbar of Oncourse CL. Learn how to upload and send attachments.

- Check with your instructor or read your R110 syllabus regarding the use of Oncourse CL in your class. Ask questions if you don't understand how it will be used.

- Some instructors may opt to test or quiz you by using the Test and Survey Tool. Please read about online testing integrity in the Policies and Procedures section of this Coursebook.

TIME MANAGEMENT

Every new semester looms ahead like a clean art canvas. Sometimes the emptiness of a new project can be overwhelming. You need to start **early** on your masterpiece—bit by bit. This is not a course that you can cram for. You can't stay up all night and put together a speech—not without disastrous results.

Look at your syllabus. You'll see that your assignments have been placed in a deliberate building-block arrangement. You will also note that the later speeches have been weighted more heavily. This is because as you approach the end of the semester you should be prepared to pull in more sophisticated techniques employed by good speakers. So more will be asked of you.

Read each assignment carefully. Pay careful attention to the requirements and criteria listed. Note the date on your syllabus that you will give your speech. Work backwards to allow yourself enough time to get the job done. You'll get a handle on the amount of time needed as you listen to your instructor and discuss the assignment.

Give yourself time to think. Choosing the right topic is key to success. Be sure you feel comfortable with your topic before proceeding. Then allow yourself time to fail. Yes, fail. What happens if that perfect topic just falls apart? You realize that your audience analysis won't allow you to do that topic, or you find that you can't find the material you wanted. Whatever the reason, you need to have enough time that you can afford a day's setback. Then when you start over, you won't panic. You'll be in control and know that you still have the time needed to do a good job.

After choosing the topic and preparing your audience analysis, look at the task checklist. Use it as a guide and check off each job as you get it done. There's a tremendous satisfaction gained as you move through the semester and master each requirement.

If you approach your speech assignments with a plan in mind, you'll have a better handle on what you need to accomplish. Keep that flexible attitude and remember to update any changes in your syllabus as they occur. Break each speech assignment down into smaller chunks and put them in your planner/calendar. **Be diligent about your tasks.** If you approach each speech as a huge endeavor, it will be. Instead keep that timeline in mind and check off those smaller jobs.

How well you do this semester is strictly up to you. Your instructor will be there to support you. If you experience problems, bring them to your instructor and hear what they have to say. Asking questions in advance will only help you later. Using your time well is an integral part of succeeding as a public speaker. Take every edge you can. Create a masterpiece!

A Word About "Criticism"

According to student surveys and conversations with students it becomes very clear that one thing that concerns you is the "criticism" you will receive from your teachers and classmates after you give your speeches. Although the R110 faculty chooses to regard this phenomenon as "oral evaluation," students still don't seem to be able to get rid of the connotation of "negative judgment, censure, or finding fault." **Try to remember that your teacher and classmates are not judging your worth as a person, they are evaluating your skills in public speaking.**

It is the philosophy of the R110 faculty to preserve the worth of the individual and ultimately his/her work. Therefore we regard the act of appraising speeches as one of "evaluation" which is defined as " . . . determining the worth or value of . . ." This type of appraisal carries with it your instructor's responsibility to listen accurately and to observe your speeches and determine their worth based on those observations. Remember that your instructor is working toward helping you improve your speaking abilities, and he/she should be considerably practiced in the art of oral and written evaluation. Pay close attention your teacher's comments, otherwise you may end up practicing your mistakes!

As you evaluate the speeches of your peers, the same thing applies. You are responsible for listening ethically, observing behaviors, and evaluating content in a way that will help the speaker become a more effective communicator. If you are a good listener and a discerning thinker, you will become a more effective speech evaluator. The author of your text, Stephen Lucas, gives you an excellent background in ethical listening and thinking techniques in Chapters 2 & 3. It is your responsibility to pay close attention to these chapters because they will help you to be more "evaluative" and less "judgmental" in your appraisal of others. This is a skill that translates to many other areas of your life.

So, when you think about the part of this class where your classmates and instructor tell you what they think about your speech, look forward to it as an "evaluative" experience when the "worth" of your speech is discussed and you learn to improve your speaking skills from that discussion. This is a necessary process in the art of public speaking.

LIBRARY

General information is available for both Indianapolis and Columbus by accessing:

<http://www.iupui.edu/libraries.htm>

General information by phone: Indianapolis: (317) 274-8278

Columbus: (812) 348-7222 or

1-800-414-8782

(from 8:00 a.m. to 5:00 p.m.)

Call ahead or check the web to verify hours.

Library Research and Resources for IUPUI and IUPU Columbus

By Bill Orme
IUPUI University Library

While much of the information you gather for your speeches may come from your own knowledge, experience or contacts, you will likely need to call upon other resources for background information, current trends, or perspectives other than your own. The Internet is a valuable tool, and should definitely be considered a resource, but other more traditional resources are also available within your campus libraries, which may serve your needs as well as, or even better than the Internet.

Before you begin to conduct research in the library, ask yourself two questions: "What kind of information will I need?" and "What tools do I need to know how to use to get that information?"

Determining Your Information Needs

Be sure to read Chapter 4 of *The Art of Public Speaking* before you begin any library research. Coming to the library with a **specific purpose statement in mind** will allow you to make more efficient use of your time. You will be able to ask more informed questions as you seek help from librarians, and you will be better able to focus your research. If you are having difficulty arriving at a specific purpose statement, consult your instructor. Make sure your instructor has approved your topic before you research it thoroughly.

The type of information you need and, to some extent, the resources you need to consult, will be determined by your specific purpose statement. Your textbook shows several examples of effective and ineffective purpose statements, including these:

Ineffective: To persuade my audience that something should be done about the federal budget deficit.

More Effective: To persuade my audience that a national sales tax should be instituted to help reduce the federal budget deficit.

The more effective purpose statement allows you to avoid researching "the federal budget deficit", an extremely large topic which would yield an immense amount of information, and to focus instead on information about a national sales tax. In this case your research might concentrate on past (or current) proposals of this sort, the arguments pro and con, and any case studies in which other countries have adopted such a tax. Now that you have a focus for your research you can begin to identify sources which are likely to produce the kinds of information you need.

Beginning Library Research

A university library can be an intimidating place. It is typically large and full of unfamiliar resources. There is commonly a temptation to fall back on your local public library to meet your information needs. Unfortunately, the public library is not generally equipped to meet the needs of university students. The university library, however, concentrates on meeting the information needs of the university's students and faculty members.

Before you *need* to use the library, go look at it. Find out what it looks like. Discover where things are. Where is the reference section? Where are the magazines? What kinds of special collections are in the library? What kinds of computers do they have available? Where can I get help? Which areas of the library offer what kinds of assistance? Half an hour spent exploring the library at your leisure can be a wonderful investment. It certainly beats trying to figure these questions out while trying to beat a deadline!

Before you *have to* use the library, try to figure out how some of the basic tools work. Try to do some searches in the library's catalog. Look up your favorite author. Try to find a book you have already read. Look up a broad topic, and then try to narrow it. Ask the librarian to help you find articles on something you are interested in. Pay attention to the resources they suggest. Playing with these resources ahead of time will make it easier to work with them later.

When you do get ready to use the library for your research, plan to spend some time there. Block out an hour or so. Don't be in a hurry. If at all possible, come to the library in the off-hours, early in the morning or in the evening when it is less crowded. Don't be shy! Librarians are paid to answer your questions. Keep in mind, though, that you have a responsibility as a university student to become an independent learner. This means you should try to find your own answers before you ask for help. Librarians will offer guidance, but you are ultimately responsible for deciding what information you will use in your work.

University Library Resources

This is a selective list of resources available within or through the University Library. Some of the items included on this list have special features.

 indicates titles mentioned in *The Art of Public Speaking.*

 indicates resources that are available electronically. If you want to use these resources, go to *<http://www.ulib.iupui.edu/u110/indexes.html>* and you will be provided with direct links.

 indicates items which are available online from inside University Library only.

 indicates items that are available in print format only.

- Library call numbers are listed in parentheses immediately after the title of the work. All works with call numbers will be found in the IUPUI University Library reference collection on the 2nd floor.

- Most of the resources listed are also available in the IUPU Columbus Library. Those with call numbers are located in the Columbus Library reference collection.

General Indexes

 Academic Search Elite. Provides abstracts and indexing for over 3,400 scholarly journals covering the social sciences, humanities, education and more. Also offers full-text for over 2,000 journals with many dating back to 1985. Includes coverage of over 1,500 peer-reviewed journals.

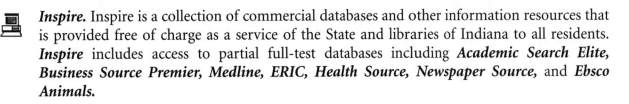 ***IngentaConnect.*** IngentaConnect provides keyword access to information from the tables of contents of over 29,000 journals, including 8,000 online. IngentaConnect includes periodicals from all subject areas, but concentrates heavily on the sciences and social sciences.

Expanded Academic ASAP. This database provides access to 3,500 indexed and full-text titles, including 2,100 peer-reviewed journals, covering all disciplines dating back to 1985. This index is especially useful to find information on astronomy, religion, law, history, psychology, the humanities, current events, sociology, communications and the general sciences.

 Inspire. Inspire is a collection of commercial databases and other information resources that is provided free of charge as a service of the State and libraries of Indiana to all residents. *Inspire* includes access to partial full-test databases including ***Academic Search Elite, Business Source Premier, Medline, ERIC, Health Source, Newspaper Source,*** and ***Ebsco Animals.***

 Readers' Guide to Periodical Literature. (A13.R48) An author/subject index to selected general interest periodicals of reference value in libraries dating back to 1900.

 Readers' Guide Retrospective. An online version of ***Readers' Guide to Periodical Literature*** that covers the years 1890–1982.

Special Indexes

 Applied Science and Technology Full Text. Periodical coverage includes trade and industrial publications, journals issued by professional and technical societies, and specialized subject periodicals, as well as special issues such as buyers' guides, directories, and conference proceedings. Abstracting coverage begins with periodicals published in March 1993. The abstracts range from 50 to 300 words and describe the content and scope of the source articles. Full Text coverage begins in 1997.

 Art Full Text. Art Full Text is a bibliographic database that indexes and abstracts articles from periodicals published throughout the world. Full-text coverage for selected periodicals is also included. Indexing coverage begins 1984; abstracting coverage begins with January 1994. The abstracts range from 50 to 300 words and describe the content and scope of the source articles. Full-text coverage begins in 1997.

Business Source Premier. Full text for more than 8,800 serials, including articles concerning business, management, finance, trade, new technologies, trends.

 Education Full Text. Articles concerning preschool, elementary, secondary and higher education, special and vocational education, comparative and multicultural education, adult and continuing education, and computer technology. Abstracting coverage begins with January 1994. Abstracts range from 50 to 300 words and describe the content and scope of the source documents. Full-text coverage begins in January 1996.

ERIC (Education Resources Information Center). Summaries of articles concerning education and related disciplines.

Ethnic News Watch. Full-text articles on national and international topics of interest from ethnic, minority, and native presses.

 Humanities Full Text. Articles concerning classical studies, philosophy, and religion. Periodical coverage includes some of the best-known scholarly journals and numerous lesser-known but important specialized magazines. Full-text coverage begins in January 1995.

Social Sciences Index. (AI3.R5) Indexes over 200 scholarly, English language journals in the social sciences.

Newspapers

 LEXIS/NEXIS Academic. Full-text articles from newspapers concerning business, news, government, finance, law and legislation.

 Indianapolis Star. The last seven days of Indianapolis Star is available online at IndyStar.com. University Library holds this newspaper in paper and microfilm back to 1907.

New York Times. The current issue of the New York Times is available online via University Library. The ***Historical New York Times*** is an online version of the newspaper dating from 1851 to 2003.

Wall Street Journal. The print version of the Wall Street Journal from 1959 to the present is available at University Library. The library also provides an online version of the newspaper that goes back to 1984.

 Washington Post. The Washington Post is available in microfilm and print back to 1975.

Encyclopedias

 Britannica Online. Online version of the Encyclopedia Britannica.

Encyclopedia of Bioethics. (REF QH332.E52 2004). Collections of scholarly articles on the core areas of bioethics.

 Concise Routledge Encyclopedia of Philosophy. Available online through ebrary and NetLibrary.

Encyclopedia of Religion (BL31.E46 2005)

New Grove Encyclopedia of Music and Musicians ML100.G885 2001

Grzimek's Animal Life Encyclopedia (REF QL3.G7813 2003)

McGraw-Hill Encyclopedia of Science & Technology (REF Q121.M3 2002)

Yearbooks

 Facts on File: Weekly World News (REF D410 .F3) An online weekly loose-leaf world news digest with cumulative index provided as a part of *LEXIS/NEXIS Academic.*

 Statistical Abstract of the United States (C 3.134:) Please note that this item is kept at the Reference Desk.

World Almanac and Book of Facts (REF AY67.N5 W7) Also available electronically through EbscoHost.

World Factbook. (Prex 3.15) Published by the Central Intelligence Agency. The current edition is available at University Library's Reference Desk.

Dictionaries

 Merriam-Webster Online Dictionary and Thesaurus. Online version of Merriam Webster's Collegiate dictionary.

 Oxford English Dictionary(OED Online)

Quotation Books

Familiar Quotations. (REF PN6081 .B27 2002) Also known as **Bartlett's Quotations,** the most recent edition is kept behind the Reference Desk. Also available online.

Harper Book of American Quotations (REF PN6084.A5 C37 1988).

My Soul Looks Back, 'less I Forget: a Collection of Quotations by People of Color (REF PN6081.3.M9 1993)

New Quotable Woman (REF PN6081.5.N49 1992).

Oxford Dictionary of Quotations (REF PN6080.095 2004).

Biographical Aids

Biography.com. Produced by the Biography Channel. Biographical information on over 25,000 celebrities and people of reknown.

Biography Resource Center. Biographical information from Gale reference books and full-text periodical articles.

Current Biography (REF CT100.C8)

International Who's Who (REF CT120.I5)

Literature Resource Center. Available online. Includes information from Contemporary Authors.

Who's Who in America (REF E176.W642)

Who's Who of American Women (REF E176.W647)

Atlases and Gazetteers

Atlas of the World (REF G1021.A7545 2004). Please note that this item is kept in an atlas case in the reference area.

Commercial Atlas and Marketing Guide (REF HF1023.R18) Please note that this item is kept in an atlas case in the reference area.

Goode's World Atlas (REF G1019 .G67 1995).

National Atlas of the United States. Available online through University Library's "Quick Reference Resources" link.

Library Catalogs

 IUCAT. The online library catalog for the entire IU Library system. Books, videos, and journals are searchable by author, title, periodical title, subject and keyword. Includes a link to MY ACCOUNT which allows users to renew library materials online.

 Indianapolis-Marion County Public Library. The online catalog for the Marion county public library.

 Purdue University. The online catalog to the libraries at Purdue West Lafayette.

 Other Academic Libraries in Indiana. Links to the online catalog of Ball State, Notre Dame and other Indiana academic libraries.

 Library of Congress. The online catalog at the Library of Congress.

Contributions by
Janet Feldmann, Director of Library and Media Services, Emerita, IUPU Columbus
and by Steven Schmidt, Director of Library and Media Services, University Library.
Revised by William Orme, 2006

EVALUATING SOURCES OF INFORMATION ON THE WEB*

*For an interesting and challenging exercise in Website evaluation, see the "Comparing and Contrasting Websites" exercise in the Appendix of this book.

- **Author**
  Who is the author/creator of the web page? What is her/his occupation, position, education, experience, etc.? Is the author/creator qualified to write the homepage?

- **Purpose**
  What is the purpose for creating the homepage?

- **Author Bias**
  Does the author/creator have a bias or make assumptions on which the information contained in the homepage rests? What are they?

- **Information Source**
  What method of obtaining the data, or conducting the research was employed by the author/creator? Is the homepage based on personal opinion or experience, interviews, library research, questionnaires, etc.?

- **Author Conclusion**
  At what conclusion does the author/creator arrive?

- **Conclusion Justification**
  Does the author/creator satisfactorily justify the conclusion from the research or experience? Why or why not?

- **Relationship to Other Works**
  How does this homepage compare with similar works (books, journals articles, etc.)? Is it in tune with or in opposition to conventional wisdom, established scholarship, professional practice, governmental policy, etc.? Are there specific studies, writings, schools of thought, philosophies, etc., with which this one agrees or disagrees of which you should be aware?

- **Significant Attachments**
  Are there significant attachments or appendices such as charts, maps, bibliographies, photos, documents, tests or questionnaires? If not, should there be?

- **Currency of Homepage**
  Is the homepage dated as to when it was created or last updated? Is the data current on the homepage? Is the homepage stable?

Based on a handout created by Eugene Engeldinger, Director of Library Services, Carthage College. Revised for the World Wide Web by Sharon Hay, Assistant Librarian, IUPUI.

POPULAR MAGAZINES AND SCHOLARLY JOURNALS

How to Tell the Difference

	Magazines	Journals
Purpose?	Entertainment/News; General information	Communication of research findings
Intended Audience?	General public	Written for professional colleagues
Distribution?	Newsstands; general subscriptions	Membership subscriptions
Advertising?	Many ads for popular items	Few ads for professional items
Publisher?	Commercial publisher	Academic publisher
Frequency?	Fairly frequent (weekly/monthly)	Fairly infrequent (monthly/quarterly)
Tone/Language?	Engaging/Sensational; Easy to read and understand	Serious/Scholarly; Technical language/Professional jargon
Graphics?	Many illustrations; Photographs; Often in color	Few illustrations; Charts/Graphs; Often black & white
Depth of Coverage?	General information about a topic; Shorter articles	More detailed, technical information; Current research reported; Longer articles
Sources Cited?	Rarely	Footnotes and bibliographies
Authors?	Credentials rarely given; May not have knowledge in the field	Professional position and affiliation listed; Typically experts in the area

Adapted 5/98/William Orme

THE SPEAKER'S LAB

Cavanaugh Hall Basement - Room 001G

Help with:

Technology   *Content*   *Practice*

The Speaker's Lab is available for use by all students, but is especially designed to help R110 students. In the Speaker's Lab students will be provided the opportunity to fine-tune their speeches with the aid of student mentors and a host of technological equipment.

Three studios are available for practicing speeches. Each studio is equipped with all the supplies needed to:

- Practice a speech
- Time a speech
- Practice with any visual aids, including:
  - PowerPoint
  - Document cameras
  - Video
- Record a practice
- Review taped speeches, with or without a mentor
- Larger practice room for group presentation.

Students may also meet one-on-one with a student mentor about other areas in the speech-making process such as brainstorming, outlining, and research. Technological guidance is also available for those struggling with images or PowerPoint.

Speaker's Lab hours maybe found outside of CA001G or on the Speaker's Lab webpage. Open M-S

Appointments (317–278–7940 or <spchlab@iupui.edu>)

You must make an appointment to visit the Speaker's Lab. Although walk-ins are sometimes possible, scheduled appointments always take priority. Call, e-mail, or visit the Speaker's Lab to make an appointment.

Reminders

- ■ The Speaker's Lab is not a substitute for going to class or working with your instructor.
- ■ You should come prepared to work on something when you visit the lab
- ■ Bring: A videotape, if you wish to record your presentation.
  - • This Coursebook (speech assignment)
  - • Any outlines or notes you have
  - • Your section number (we will use this to inform your instructor of your visit)

Staff

The Speaker's Lab is staffed with a lab coordinator, technical consultants, and student mentors. The student mentors have already taken and done well in R110. If you are interested in becoming a mentor, you must have taken R110 and earned a minimum grade of "B+," have excellent interpersonal skills, a working knowledge of available technology, a desire to help others and a recommendation from your R110 instructor. Call 317-278-7940 for more information.

| Spchlab@iupui.edu | <http://liberalarts.iupui.edu/spchlab> | (317) 278-7940 |

COMPUTER LAB INFORMATION

Indianapolis:

Hours for on-campus computer labs can be obtained by using:

<http://www.iupui.edu/~stctr>

This page will provide you with phone numbers, hours of operation, application software, multimedia hardware availability, and room reservation procedures. In addition, you may call UITS at (317) 274-7383.

Columbus:

For computer lab locations and hours of operation, visit the IUPUC computer lab website at:

<http://www.iupuc.edu/cptlab>

Tech support is available through Kyle Leach at the Computer Lab. You can reach him at (812) 348-7239 or *<leachmk@purdue.edu>*.

Technology Support–IUPUI

General information about University Information Technology Services can be obtained by accessing the following web pages:

For technology services and support see *<http://uits.iu.edu>*.

Powerpoint Training

Students in R110 **are required** to become familiar with PowerPoint. In addition to being available in all public labs, a recent version of PowerPoint can be downloaded for use on your personally owned computer for **free** at *<http://iuware.iu.edu>*. Although R110 Instructors will provide various ways for students to learn and practice PowerPoint for use in their R110 speeches, students are invited to seek PowerPoint training on their own by signing up for **free STEPS** classes at *<http://ittraining.iu.edu>* or by calling 317-274-7383. See your instructor's syllabus for other information regarding PowerPoint training.

Columbus students: See Computer Lab Information section of this Coursebook.

PowerPoint Transparencies

IUPUI Only

You may not generate color or black and white transparencies on campus. There are many copy shops in the area that can accommodate your needs (PIP, Kinkos, etc.). Make sure you have your original with you. If the shop has to pull up your work on a disk, they will charge you more money to access and print your slides.

IUPU Columbus Only

Color transparencies cannot be made on campus, but are available at Mail Boxes Etc. in Columbus. Color, of course, would be preferable. However, if that is not possible, your instructor will accept black only. These can be made on campus.

QUESTIONNAIRE ON TECHNICAL SKILLS

Name: _____   Section #: _____

Circle the MOST appropriate response for you in relation to these various technical areas.

I am . . .	Very Comfortable (VC) Somewhat Comfortable (SC) Not Comfortable (NC)		
Word processing on a computer.	VC	SC	NC
Using PowerPoint.	VC	SC	NC
Adding pictures to PowerPoint.	VC	SC	NC
Communicating via e-mail.	VC	SC	NC
Sending attachments by e-mail.	VC	SC	NC
Accessing the Internet.	VC	SC	NC
Searching for information on the Internet.	VC	SC	NC
Finding images via the Internet.	VC	SC	NC
Using Oncourse CL.	VC	SC	NC
Communicating with classmates via e-mail or forums within Oncourse CL.	VC	SC	NC
Storing files within "Resources" of Oncourse CL.	VC	SC	NC
Taking tests or surveys on Oncourse CL.	VC	SC	NC
Searching electronic databases in a library.	VC	SC	NC

Circle the MOST appropriate response for you in relation to these various areas.

I am . . .	Very Comfortable (VC) Somewhat Comfortable (SC) Not Comfortable (NC)		
Writing a research paper.	VC	SC	NC
Creating a works cited page.	VC	SC	NC
Citing references within a research paper.	VC	SC	NC
Finding student resources available to help me on campus.	VC	SC	NC

Created by Stephen Lebeau, Jr. Coordinator of the IUPUI Speaker's Lab, IUPUI Liberal Arts Technical Services.

WRITING CENTER SUPPORT

As you prepare your outlines and other written materials, you may choose to have someone look over your work and get some writing advice from an outside source. The Writing Centers at both Indianapolis and Columbus offer services that could help you with your written assignments. It might be a question of getting help with brainstorming, grammar, or the strategy of developing your outline. Whatever the question, you should go to the professionals for help. They are there to help you with all of your writing needs.

Indianapolis

The University Writing Center is located in Cavanaugh Hall Room 427 and University Library, UL 2125 and is staffed by English faculty and experienced students. You can sign up for tutoring in CA 427 by calling 317-274-2049 or in UL 2125 at 317-278-8171.

You can find out more about the University Writing Center by visiting their homepage at:

<http://www.iupui.edu/~uwc/>

You also can get quick questions answered about grammar, usage, punctuation and documentation by calling the UWC HOTLINE at 317-278-9999 during regular business hours.

Columbus

The Writing Center is located in the main building adjacent to Student Services. The phone number is (812) 348-7269. Appointments are available in half-hour increments and a sign up sheet is posted outside the Center with the names and available time slots of the peer tutors.

MLA Documentation

Your research should be documented using the Modern Language Association style. Samples of proper documentation style of different types of sources are also available in the CDROM that comes with your textbook. The **BiblioMaker,** on CDROM #1, in Bibliographical Formats, will help you to format your source citations. If you have additional questions, you may find the MLA Website handy. Their web address is: *<http://www.mla.org>*. Also, see MLA Guidelines in The Preparation Outline section of this book.

STUDENT INFORMATION SHEET

Name _____

Address _____

_____

_____

Home Phone _____ Work/Cell Phone _____ IM name _____ (opt.)

E-Mail _____ Age _____ Yr. In School _____

List other classes you are taking this semester: _____

_____

_____

List extra-curricular activities you are currently involved in: _____

_____

_____

Are you currently working full or part-time? _____ How many hours day/week? _____

Where are you currently working? _____

What language(s) do you speak? _____

List any public speaking experiences you have had. Include teaching, taking other speech courses, and the giving of major presentations.

_____

_____

_____

_____

_____

_____

_____

Student Contract

I, _____, have read the general rules in the Coursebook and my instructor's syllabus for the R110 class. I understand all of the policies and procedures, the work, preparation and performance expected in the class and agree to abide by those policies, procedures and expectations. I also understand the attendance policy and the penalties for missing class time.

I understand that R110 participates in the University policy of Administrative Withdrawal (See Policies and Procedures.) I understand that if I am withdrawn from R110 that it can have academic, financial, and financial aid implications. It is my understanding that Administrative Withdrawal takes place after the full refund period, and if I am withdrawn from the course I will not be eligible for a tuition refund.

I also understand that the instructors of R110 utilize the services of Turnitin.com in order to discourage plagiarism in the creation of student speeches and other written assignments. By signing this student contract I agree to upload written assignments to the R110 portal on Turnitin.com, as directed by my R110 instructor.

_____   _____
Signature   Date

SPEECH NIGHT—IUPUI

Created by Drs. David Burns and B. Bruce Wagener in 1971, Speech Night has been a Communication Studies Department tradition that showcases the skill and talent of R110 students. **Speech Night is as integral to the R110 course as are speeches and exams.** *All students and teachers* **are required to participate on some level, whether it be managing, judging, speaking or listening.**

Each semester (except summer) the R110 faculty conducts a semi-final contest of persuasive speeches by having their student select a speaker from each section of R110. Student judges are named and given the opportunity to select a winner from each of the semi-final rounds. The following week, these winners go on to a final round and R110 faculty who do not have a student in the final round determine the winner.

Certificates are awarded to all students who compete. Medals are awarded to all finalists and trophies to the first, second and third place contestants. Beginning in the fall of 1998, the *B. Bruce Wagener Award in Public Speaking* will be given to the first place winner, courtesy of McGraw-Hill Custom Publishing. This award has monetary value and honors the co-creator of Speech Night.

■ SPEECH NIGHT *SEMI-FINALS* WILL BE HELD ON _____ at **7:30 P.M. sharp** in the _____ Building. *Judges and speakers* must be there at 7:15 sharp. Judges who show up after rounds begin will not be able to judge. Late speakers will be worked into the speaking schedule.

■ SPEECH NIGHT *FINALS* WILL BE HELD ON _____ in _____ at **7:30 P.M. sharp.** *Audience members* should be in their seats by 7:30 P.M. Finalists must arrive at the speaking venue no later than 7 P.M.

Here are the rules for Speech Night contestants:

1. Student speakers must be enrolled in R110 and selected by classmates in their section.

2. The nominee must enter the contest with a 6 1/2–7 1/2 minute persuasive speech on a question of policy. *No exceptions.* **The speech must follow the *Monroe Motivated Sequence.***

3. Speeches under 6 1/2 and over 7 1/2 will be penalized during the contests.

4. Students may have transparencies, posters, objects or very short video or audiotapes for speaking aids. **Computers and LCD equipment with PowerPoint will be available in each semi-find room.**

5. No more than 3 note cards may be used. (3″ × 5″ or 4″ × 6″) No manuscripts are allowed!

Here are the rules for non-speakers:

1. **Attending Speech Night finals is a required activity** and, unless you have a conflicting class, you are required to attend Speech Night FINALS. If you can't participate in Speech Night in some way, your instructor will provide another activity for you to make up for your absence at this event.

2. Because of space limitations **students are NOT allowed to observe semi-final rounds for purposes of doing Outside Speaker Reports.** You must be a judge or speaker to be present in a semi-final round.

3. Some of **you may want to be judges at semifinals.** Students have told us that this is a very interesting and educational activity—fun, even! Ask your instructor.

4. You are **expected to be good listeners** at Speech Night Finals. You are also expected to give honest feedback and cheer for your favorite speaker. You are expected to be polite and not talk during speeches. **Cell phones and beepers are to be turned off during the event.**

5. Attendance will be taken by instructors at the end of the contest.

POLICIES AND PROCEDURES

Policies and Procedures
Procedures for Academic Conflict Resolution IUPUI

Policies and Procedures

Attendance

Read This Carefully, Please.

Your attendance at all scheduled R110 classes is desired and required. ***Attendance in R110 classes is mandatory.*** Our reasoning is simple: learning to listen effectively is one of the learning objectives in the class and it, along with interpersonal communication, is crucial to the effectiveness of the R110 learning environment. **Therefore, our policy may be stricter than the attendance policies of your classes in other departments.** Please remember that this is because critical listening and participating is crucial to your skill development in the field of communication. **If you are not in class, you will not have the opportunity to improve your skills.**

However, we do realize that "stuff happens," so we have implemented the following attendance policy:

Fall and Spring Semesters

You are allowed 2 absences in a 2-day/wk class and 1 absence in a class that meets one time per week. These absences will be recorded without judgment except in the following cases: 1) You may **not** be absent on the day you are scheduled to speak and, 2) you may not be absent on a day you have other in-class responsibilities such as peer evaluations or anything else determined by your instructor. This means that if you are absent after you have already accrued the maximum number of absences, you will be required to have official documentation for that absence (doctor, hospital, lawyer, police, etc.). Official documents **cannot** be used to excuse either of the first two absences accrued. Absences with documentation that occur after the first two must be judged as beyond the student's control. **See your instructor's syllabus for details regarding the consequences of your absences. Keep in mind our absence policy is designed for personal emergencies. Utilize your absences wisely, if at all!**

(For sports-related absences and other special accommodations, see next section.)

Summer Sessions

Only **ONE** absence is allowed during either of the summer sessions. Other attendance rules as stated above still apply.

Tardiness

Your instructor needs to begin class promptly at the scheduled time. If you are tardy for any reason, you will be marked as such, whether you are late or leave early (see you instructor's policy.)

Administrative Withdrawal

All R110 sections participate in a program allowing teachers to automatically withdraw a student who has not attended at least 50% of the first 4 weeks of class. Although there is an appeal process associated with this policy, we strongly urge you to keep in touch with your instructor through email or phone should you have circumstances which would prevent you from being in class during the first four weeks. Otherwise, you will be eliminated from the class roster and be unable to complete the course.

Please note that administrative withdrawal may have academic, financial, and financial aid implications. Administrative withdrawal will take place after the full refund period, so if you are administratively withdrawn from the course you will not be eligible for a tuition refund. Please note that if you accrue three Withdrawals within the first three semesters at IUPUI, you can essentially make yourself ineligible for financial aid. This is very serious. You can read more about Administrative Withdrawal at: *http://registrar.iupui.edu/withdrawal-policy.html.*

Special Accommodations

Athletic: Any student athlete competing on or managing any team is required to present the R110 instructor with a competition schedule during the first week of classes. The instructor may or may not sign the competition schedule. If the instructor signs the competition schedule, the instructor agrees to work with the student athlete on making up any missed class work due to a scheduled competition. If the student athlete does not present a competition schedule to the instructor during the first week of class, the instructor is under no obligation to accommodate the student athlete for class work or time missed.

Adaptive Educational Services: Any student having any special academic needs falling under the jurisdiction of Adaptive Educational Services (AES) must register with AES. R110 instructors will accommodate special needs students who present an official letter from AES. If you have questions regarding AES, you may contact that office at 274-3241; CA 001E. On the Columbus campus contact: Kenn Amberger *(kgamberg@iupuc.edu).* His phone number is 812/348-7252

Grading

Unless otherwise modified by your instructor, the following guidelines will be used for grading:

Oral Work:	**May include speeches, group work, class participation**	**50%**
Written: Work:	**May include outlines, tests, quizzes, outside speaker reports, audience analyses, self-evaluation, listening sheets, etc.**	**50%**

See Your Instructor's Grading Policy For A Complete Explanation.

Incomplete Grade

A grade of "I" may only be awarded only in extraordinary circumstances:

Criteria are as follows:

1. If the student has completed at least 75% of the required work in the course.

2. If the student has a "passing" (A, B, C, D) grade on the 75% or more that has been completed.

3. If the reason for the inability to finish was completely beyond the student's control.

4. If the student notified the instructor personally.

5. If the notification to the instructor was made promptly and with little delay.

Speaking Time and Overtime

1. You must learn to **plan** for a certain time; you must learn to recognize your "expansion" rate from outline to notes.

2. You must realize that the time accorded you is not a gift of the audience, but an expectation.

3. Because of the short speaking time in class, going over the set time limit takes away from the speaking time of other students who are ready to speak that day.

4. In the same way, overtime takes away time for questions and criticism from the class and the instructor.

THEREFORE, penalties will be levied by your instructor when you speak either *under* or *over* the specified time requirement.

Academic Integrity

From the SLA Bulletin 1998–2000 (page 20):

Cheating: Cheating is dishonesty of any kind with respect to examinations, course assignments, alteration of records, or illegal possession of examinations, regardless of how they are delivered (electronically, hard copy, etc.) It is the responsibility of the student not only to abstain from cheating, but in addition, to avoid the appearance of cheating and to guard against making it possible for others to cheat. Any student who helps another student cheat is as guilty of cheating as the student assisted. The student should do everything possible to induce respect for the examining process and for honesty in the performance of assigned tasks in or out of class.

Plagiarism: Plagiarism is the offering of the work of someone else as one's own. Honesty requires that any ideas or materials taken from another source for either written or oral use must be fully acknowledged. The language or ideas taken from another may range from isolated formulas, sentences, or paragraphs to entire articles copied from books, periodicals, speeches, or the writings of other students. The offering of materials assembled or collected by others in the form of projects or collections without acknowledgment is also considered plagiarism. Any student who fails to give credit for ideas or materials taken from another source is guilty of plagiarism.

Checking For Integrity

IUPUI has contracted with Turnitin.com so that instructors have access to an electronic tool to check your outlines and papers for accuracy and originality. Your instructor will talk about plagiarism in class and it is covered extensively in your text, *The Art of Public Speaking* by Stephen Lucas. You will be asked by your instructor to log onto Turnitin.com and create a user profile. Your instructor will supply you a Class ID as well as a Turnitin Class Enrollment password so that you will have access to your instructor's R110 node on Turnitin.com. All outlines must be uploaded to Turnitin as well as other written assignments as directed by your instructor. *Your cooperation will help to insure that others do not seek to copy your hard work.*

We take Academic Integrity very seriously here at IUPUI and in the Communication Studies department. Our participation in the Turnitin program in R110 reflects our commitment to eliminate plagiarism and to provide discipline for those students who plagiarize. Additional information about the tool can be found at: http://turnitin.com.

A faculty member who has evidence that a student is guilty of cheating or plagiarism shall initiate the process of determining the student's guilt or innocence. No penalty shall be imposed until the student has been informed of the charge and of the evidence on which it is based and has been given an opportunity to present a defense. If the faculty member finds the student guilty, the faculty member assesses the penalty within the course and promptly reports the case in writing to the Dean of the school or comparable head of the academic unit. The report should include the names of any other students who may be involved in the incident and recommendations for further action. The Dean, in consultation with the faculty member if the latter so desires, will initiate any further disciplinary proceedings and inform the faculty member of any action taken. In every case, a record of the offenses remains of file in the Office of the Dean.

Some Key Rules

1. Organization must always be original.

2. Ideas and phrases may, of course, be quoted so long as each quoted item is clearly identified as such when it is given. Quoting any phrases or ideas without removing the implication that they are original with you is plagiarism.

3. Give specific citations, not "blanket" ones. For example:

    Right: "This 'public washroom school of fiction' as *Newsweek* called it, is all too popular." (This student clearly identifies the quoted item as it is given, and gives the specific source citation.)

    Wrong: "Several ideas and phrases in this speech have been taken from George Bernard Shaw." (Which ideas? Which works by Shaw?)

Online Testing Integrity

Your instructor may use the Oncourse Test and Survey Tool to test you in an unproctored setting. You need to make sure that you are conforming to the classroom standards for academic honesty when you take the test or quiz. Keep in mind that if there are similarities in time, score and IP address of any pairs or groups of students, you may be called to account for these similarities.

Your teacher will be able to tell you what you should do if your computer crashes or the test was compromised in any way by a technological crisis. BE SURE TO CHECK WITH YOUR INSTRUCTOR REGARDING HIS/HER POLICIES ON THIS MATTER.

Written Assignment Requirements

- **All written materials must be typed or word-processed.** The sheets needed to complete each assignment can be found later in this coursebook. Check each assignment for the exact materials needed. Use your task checklist and mark off each item as you complete it. Make sure that you bring all the correct items with you on your assigned speaking day.

Materials Needed

- Lucas, Stephen E. *The Art Of Public Speaking*, 9th Edition, and accompanying CD-ROMs. Boston, MA, McGraw-Hill Publishing, 2005.

- Cochrane, Fox, Thedwall. *The R110 Student Coursebook*, 10th Edition. Boston, MA, McGraw-Hill Custom Publishing, 2007.

- One 90-minute clean, dedicated videotape of high quality, please.

- One pack of 3 × 5 or 4 × 6 white index cards.

- Other materials as required by your instructor.

Unacceptable Materials and Behaviors

Due to their illegal nature and the possibility of physical harm, **the following materials are not** permitted to be brought into the classroom either for inclusion in speeches or for other purposes:

1. Firearms, knives, or any other personal weapons commonly used in hand-to-hand violence.

2. Fireworks, incendiary devices or other dangerous explosives.

3. Illegal drugs or controlled substances.

4. Alcoholic beverages.

5. Swords.

6. Arrows.

7. Live or dead animals (except for service animals).

8. Pepper spray, tear gas etc.

Due to the danger to the general populace, the **following actions are not permitted** as a part of the classroom either for inclusion in speeches or for any other purposes.

1. Lewd, indecent or obscene behavior and language.

2. Knowingly making false reports or warnings concerning impending bombings, fires or other emergencies or catastrophes.

3. Disorderly conduct which interferes with the teaching and learning processes.*

4. Any actions which endanger the student, fellow students, instructor, or those present in the university community.

*Disruptive Student Behavior

IUPUI is an intellectual community dedicated to creating an environment in which individuals can succeed. Each person is important. When even one of our members is prevented from doing his or her best, the entire community is diminished. As an institution of higher learning, we must foster the best possible environment for doing our work as educators, learners, and supporters of the educational process. Therefore we are committed to the following: a) providing appropriate protection for freedom of speech and freedom of assembly, b) enhancing the opportunities for students to attain their educational objectives, c) creating and maintaining an intellectual and educational atmosphere throughout the University, and d) protecting the health, safety, welfare, property, and human rights of all members of the University and the property of the University itself.

All students are expected to be in compliance with the IUPUI *Code of Student Rights, Responsibilities, and Conduct.* This code is available at the following address: http://www.iupui.edu/code, sections G,H,I. This code is intended to promote excellence in an atmosphere of freedom and to protect the collective commitment to mutual respect in the university community. Although differences of opinion and dissent are ordinarily thought of as disagreement or debate, they are not "disruptive conduct" as long as they do not impinge upon the rights of others or interfere with the teaching/learning process in an academic setting.

When disruptive conduct occurs, our primary objective is to address the immediate problem and restore order to the classroom, office, or other academic setting.

- **Faculty, staff, and other university officials have latitude to take appropriate action as they deem necessary to maintain a positive learning environment.**

- **Faculty will follow due process, but may ask the disruptive student to leave the classroom or authorize other University officials, police or other law enforcement officials to remove the disruptive student.**

Classroom Conduct

The classroom is designed as a safe haven for all students desiring to become better, more confident public speakers. Public speaking is ranked as one of the top fears of most people, higher than the fear of death. A supportive, creative and friendly learning environment is helpful to all who are overcoming uneasiness about speaking to a group of 20 or more. It is recommended that you treat your fellow students and instructor with respect, support and courtesy throughout the semester. With everyone's cooperation, we will be able achieve an environment supportive of all.

**BEEPERS AND CELL PHONES ARE TO BE
TURNED OFF BEFORE ENTERING CLASS**

NO EXCEPTIONS.

Instructors may levy a penalty for infractions.

PROCEDURE FOR ACADEMIC CONFLICT RESOLUTION IUPUI

There may be a time during this course when you may have a disagreement with the instructor or some aspect of the course or course policy. This is normal in a performance course where your speech behaviors are constantly subject to scrutiny and evaluation. Here are some suggestions to help you through the process of resolving a problem:

1. **Work things out with your instructor first.** The best thing you can do for yourself and your teacher is to try to deal with the problem in the classroom. Going over your instructor's head without first trying to resolve the situation with him/her will antagonize your instructor unnecessarily and reduce your chances of successfully solving the problem.

2. If you are extremely upset by the situation, **calm down** before you approach your instructor. Most problems are solved logically, not emotionally.

3. **Have the facts** of the situation ready to present to your instructor.

4. If, after discussing your disagreement with your instructor, you still are not satisfied, you should **make a joint appointment** (you and your instructor) with the R110 Course Director.

5. If the problem is not resolved at the R110 Course Director level, **then the Chair** of the Department of Communication Studies will become involved.

6. To find the names, email and office addresses and phone numbers of R110 faculty and administration, go to this location on the Web. (**Note: the URL is case and space sensitive and should be typed in** *exactly* **as indicated.**)

<http://www.iupui.edu/~comstudy>

(click on R110 link)

> **NOTE:** If you elect NOT to follow the above and decide to bypass your instructor and go directly to the R110 Director or Chair, you will be referred directly back to your teacher.

THE PREPARATION OUTLINE

Required Three-Column Format for R110 Outlines
How to Cite Written Sources (MLA Guidelines)
How to Cite Source Orally (while speaking)

REQUIRED THREE-COLUMN FORMAT FOR R110 OUTLINES

The preparation outline is the blueprint of your speech. It is the visual representation of your research, your logic, your thought process and organization. You can also look at your preparation outline as a "speech plan." When you "build" your speech you will be able to "see" your speech in this preparation outline if you follow the rules of proper subordination, coordination, symbolization, and indentation. This visualization will be of great help when you create your note cards (this is your speaking outline/see chapter 10, Lucas.) Then, all you need to do is follow the "plan."

The 3-column outline is a variation on the traditional outline you see in the textbook because of the addition of a third, right-hand column. This column contains space for labeling the points where you want to give yourself directions for doing something physical. For example, if there is a point where you are to show a visual aid, then you place a "show visual aid #1" in the margin. If there is a place when you want to remind yourself to speak up or speak more slowly or to change any other vocal mechanics, the third column is a good place for you to put those directional cues. Subsequently, as you rehearse from your preparation outline, it will have the feel of a TV script, complete with directional cues. As a result, you may find it much easier to remember what you have **to say and do** while you speak.

Create a 3-column outline by downloading it from the Speaker's Lab web site (<*http://www. liberalarts.iupui.edu/spchlab*>). If you can't download the template, you can create a 3-column outline using the Tables function in Microsoft Word or similar software. You can also ask for help from the Speaker's Lab.

There are samples of student outlines using this 3-column template the Coursebook following each Speaking Assignment. Study them carefully.

The following is a sample 3-column outline template, giving you generic examples of labeling. Please refer to your speaking assignment requirements or ask your instructor for his/her labeling requirements for each speech. This is an example, only. **Although this template is realistic, it does not mean that each and every speech will contain the number of points and sub-points shown here.**

LEFT COLUMN Label speech function	MIDDLE COLUMN Content of speech *Written in Complete Sentences/Phrases*	RIGHT COLUMN Label physical behaviors and delivery cues

Specific Purpose _____

Central Idea _____

INTRODUCTION
(In Outline Form)

Attention	I.	_____	
Reveal Topic	II.	_____	(Speak slowly)
Relevancy	III.	_____	
Credibility	IV.	_____	
Preview	V.	_____	

BODY
(in outline form only)

Main Point   I. _____   (Show

Sub-Point   A. _____   Transparency #1)

         1. _____

         2. _____

Sub-Point   B. _____

         1. _____

            a. _____

            b. _____

         2. _____

Transition   (Written out in a complete sentence)

Main Point   II. _____   (Show

Sub-Point   A. _____   Transparency #2)

Sub-Point   B. _____

         1. _____

         2. _____

            a. _____

            b. _____

            c. _____

Sub-Point   C. _____

         1. _____

         2. _____

            a. _____

            b. _____

Transition		(Written out in a complete sentence)
Main Point	III.	_____
Sub-Point	A.	_____ (play tape)
Sub-Point	B.	_____
Transition (Signal End)		(Written out in a complete sentence)

INFORMATIVE CONCLUSION
(In outline form)

Restate Purpose/ Review of Main	I.	_____
Points/Circular Device	II.	_____

OR

PERSUASIVE CONCLUSION
(In outline form)

Clincher/ Exit Line/	I.	_____
Final Appeal	II.	_____

NOTE: Your instructor may have a similar version of this outline loaded into Oncourse Resources. Also, this outline template can be accessed and downloaded from the Speaker's Lab homepage: <*http://liberalarts.iupui.edu/spchlab*>. Ask your instructor for directions.

How to Cite Written Sources

Guidelines for MLA Style*

Compiled by Kelly Carter McDorman

Your outlines will require that you document your sources on the Works Cited page at the end of your outline. You are asked also to cite your sources within the outline as *in-text* or *parenthetical*. You should use MLA style of source citations on your outlines. MLA dictates what appears on your works cited page and what appears in the in-text (parenthetical) citations.

Works Cited

The list of works cited appears at the end of the outline or paper.

1. Begin the list on a new page.

2. Center the title, *Works Cited* at the top of the page.

3. Double-space between the title and the first entry.

4. Each entry should begin flush with the left margin. Indent the subsequent line/s one-half inch from the left margin.

5. The entire list should be double-spaced—both between and within entries.

6. Entries should be arranged alphabetically by author's last name or if unavailable, by the title (ignore any initial *A, An,* or *The*).

Here are sample works cited entries for common electronic sources that you will likely use. In any of the following, enclose URLs in angle brackets. Be sure you do not introduce a hyphen (or allow your word processing program to) if the URL must be divided between two lines. Break it only after a slash in the URL.

A Document within a Scholarly Project or Information Database

Citation should include:

1. Author's name (if not available, begin with title)

2. Title of work in quotation marks

3. Name of Project/Database

4. Electronic Publication Information, including version number (if relevant and not part of the title), date of electronic publication or of the last update, and name of any sponsoring institution or organization

5. Date of Access

6. URL

Examples

Huus, Kari. "Powell's Mission Impossible." *MSNBC.* 2002. MSNBC. 26 July 2002 *<http://msnbc.com/news/785591.asp>*

"This Day in History: October 9." *The History Channel Online.* 2002. History Channel 26 July 2002 *<http://historychannel.com/tdih/index.html>*

An Article in an Online Periodical

1. Author's name (if given)

2. Title of article, in quotation marks (if any; an editorial, for example, might not have a title)

3. Name of Periodical (underlined)

4. Volume number, issue number, or other identifying number

5. Date of publication

6. The number range or total number of pages, paragraphs, or other sections, if they are numbered

7. Date of access

8. URL

If all information is not available, cite what is available.

Examples

Newspaper

Shenon, Philip. "Negotiators Agree on Bill to Rewrite Bankruptcy Laws." The New York Times on the Web 26 July 2002.26 July 2002 <http://www.nytimes.com/2002/07/26/business/26BANK.html>

Magazine

Lithwick, Dahlia. "Terrorism on Trial." Slate Magazine 25 July 2002. 26 July 2002. <http://slate.msn.com//?id=2066986>.

A Professional or Personal Site

1. Person who created it (if given and relevant)

2. Title of site, underlined. (If no title, use description such as *Home page* (which may be neither underlined nor in quotation marks.)

3. The date of the last update, if given

4. The name of any organization associated with the site

5. Date of access

6. URL

Examples

Ivie, Robert L. Home page. Department of Communication and Culture, Indiana University. 26 July 2002.

National Communication Association Home Page. National Communication Association 26 July 2002 *<http://www.natcom.org>*

Article with a Printed Source/Print Analogue Accessed Electronically

1. Name of author (if given)

2. Publication information for the printed source or analogue (including title and date of print publication)

3. Title of database (underlined)

4. Publication medium (Online)

5. Name of computer service

6. Date of access

7. URL

If all information is not available, cite what is available.

Example

Weintraub, Amy. "Yoga: It's Not Just an Exercise." *Psychology Today* Nov.–Dec. 2000: 22–24. *EBSCOHost: Academic Search Full-Text Elite. Online.* 30 May 2002. *<https://proxy.ulib.iupui.edu/?url=http://search.epnet.com/login.asp>*

In-text Documentation

The Works Cited page is necessary, but not sufficient in documenting your sources. You must indicate not only what works you cited but also *precisely* what information you obtained from each source and the exact location of the material in the work. The best way to do this is with brief in-text citations (which appear within parentheses) in your outline or paper *wherever* you use another's words, facts, or ideas. Typically the author's last name and a page reference are used to indicate the source and location. An example of an in-text citation would be: (Hariman 10).

The in-text reference "(Hariman 10)" indicates the source on the alphabetically arranged list of works cited, as well as the page number.) If the author is specifically mentioned by name in the speech, then only the page number is needed, e.g. (4).

Hariman, Robert. *Political Style: The Artistry of Power.* Chicago: U of Chicago P, 1995.

1. **Guidelines**
   - In-text citations must clearly correspond to specific sources in the list of works cited.
   - Identify the location of the material as specifically as possible (page numbers, paragraph numbers, etc.)
   - The in-text citation appears before the punctuation for the sentence. It appears outside of quotation marks when the material is quoted directly.
   - Keep in-text references as brief as clarity and accuracy permit. For example, if the author's name is in the text of the outline/paper you would only need the page number in the in-text citation:

   Hariman claims that style is pivotal to policies (4).

   If the author's name wasn't in the text, it would appear in the citation:

   Style is pivotal to politics (Hariman 4).

2. **If a work is listed by title in the works cited,** page full title (if brief) or a shortened version will appear in the in-text citation before the page number.

3. **Book or article with one author (also for an interview)**

   According to Jonathan Goodwin, intellectual property attorney, the constitution affords congress the ability to grant intellectual property rights but "limits the length of the copyrights, disallowing the possibility of perpetual ownership" (29).

4. **Book or article with no author identified**

   The article "Fiscal Responsibility in Local Government" suggests staying informed by attending city council meetings and committee meetings (4)

5. **Indirect source (a quote of a quote in your source)**
   - Include the abbreviation "qtd. in" before the name of the source.
   - The example below is from an article written by Bylsma.

   Michael Irizarry, business administration professor at Texas State University, notes that capital spending for businesses "must be judged on the rate of return, not just on the revenue earned" (qtd. in Bylsma 15).

6. **Source with no page numbers (especially web pages)**
   - Print the source and cite the appropriate printed page number.
   - If only one page use (1) to assure the reader that a source is cited.

Resources

Here are some resources to help you master MLA. These resources will also indicate the works cited format for types of sources not discussed here, such as books.

1. The IUPUI Writer's Lab URL is: <*http://www.iupui.edu/~uwc*>

2. Purdue's Online Writing Lab, "OWL," has a section on MLA: <*http://owl.english.purdue.edu/handouts/research/r_mla.html*>

3. CD-ROM 1, that came with your textbook, has a section entitled "Bibliomaker". This section will help you format your citation instantly.

* Gibaldi, Joseph. *MLA Handbook for Writers of Research Papers.* 5th ed. New York: MLA of America, 1999.

How to Cite Sources Orally

Since the substance of your speech is based on research, you must be sure to cite your researched sources *orally* while you are speaking as well as throughout the preparation outline (in-text, previous section). You will be perceived as a more credible speaker when you use multiple sources and *orally* cite these sources in such a way that the audience finds them believable. Doing the actual research is only half the job in developing a speech; much of that research must be incorporated into the speech itself through citation.

When you are delivering your speeches, you should plan on telling the audience the sources of your information (book, periodical, article, web page, interview) as well as the credentials of the source (who is the author or expert, what is the author's or expert's reputation or level of expertise), while you are speaking. You cannot use information from a website, book, journal article, newspaper article, television program, radio broadcast, or any other written or spoken source, *without giving credit to the original source.* Not providing this information is considered unethical and an act of plagiarism according to the IUPUI Student Code of Ethics.

Tips on citing sources within your oral presentation

In general

- **Do not say "quote....unquote" when you offer a direct quotation. Use brief pauses to frame the quote, instead.**

- *DO NOT quote significant statistics or facts without citing where you got them!*

- **Provide enough information about each source so that your audience could, with a little effort, find it.**

- **If your source is unknown to your audience, provide enough information about your source for the audience to perceive them as credible. Typically we provide this credentialing of the source by stating the source's qualifications to discuss the topic. (See examples below)**

- **When you cite your sources, don't feel compelled always to say, "*According to* Jimmy Butler" and "*According to* Judy Kiray," and "*According to* Doris Ewing". Instead, make attempts to *vary the way in which you cite*:**

  1. "According to Judy Mack…"

  2. "A March 13th, 2006 Time magazine article by Jim Sparks mentions that…"

3. "Nancy Edwards, National Teacher of the Year suggested that students…"

4. "In a recent interview with Wayne Markwork, award winning band director at Centerville High School, emphasized the importance of…"

5. "When doing this type of operation, neurosurgeon Bryan Ludwig commented in the June 1st edition of the Indianapolis Star that…"

■ **For all sources cited and/or quoted verbally, you must note them parenthetically (in-text) on the outline and in bibliographic form on a Works Cited page. IF YOU SAY: "William Treadland, Director of the Wildlife Preservation council of Indiana, says that all Conifer trees indigenous to the state should be protected from foreign insect infestation." USE PARENTHETICAL NOTATION IN YOUR OUTLINE AS YOU WOULD FOR A WRITTEN SOURCE (Treadland 10).**

For websites

■ **When you cite a web page, do NOT say the entire address of the page, "According to www. dot redcross. dot org….". Say instead, "According to the website of the American Red Cross…."**

■ **Also, you should cite when the information on the page was last updated and any credentials that speak to the quality of information. (sponsorship or authorship and recency—Ch. 6, Lucas) See example below.**

Examples

From a book with one author:

Typically include: Author, brief credentials, date, and title

SAY: "Dr. Derek Bok, President Emeritus of Harvard University, in his 2005 book, *Our Underachieving Colleges,* wrote…"

From a book with two or more authors:

Typically include: Authors by last name, brief credentials, date, and title

SAY: "In the 1979 edition of *The Elements of Style,* renowned grammarians and composition stylists Strunk and White encourage every writer to "make every word tell.""

For a source with three, four, five, or more authors, name all authors last names in the first citation. In all subsequent citations, name only the first name listed on the source, followed by the words "et al" (Latin for "and others").

From a reference work:

Typically include: Title, credentials, and date of publication

SAY: "The 2005 edition of *Simmons Market Research*, considered by most to be the nation's leading authority on the behavior of the American consumer, notes..."

From a web site

Typically include: Site title, credentials, and date last updated (some websites may not be updated on a regular basis)

SAY: "One of the most active developers of neurotechnology, Cyberkinetics, claims on their website, last updated on March 24, 2006 that..."

From a TV or radio show:

Typically include: Name of show, date it aired, title of story, and name of reporter

SAY: "On the television show *60 Minutes* which aired on March 26, 2006, golfer Tiger Woods told reporter Ed Bradley that ..."

SAY: "On March 24, 2006, National Public Radio's *Morning Edition* aired a story by reporter Christopher Joyce entitled, "Greenland glaciers moving more quickly to the ocean." In the story, experts claimed ..."

From an interview you performed:

Typically include: Name, date, credentials

SAY: "In a personal interview conducted on February 12, 2006 with Charlotte Maddux, Director of the local chapter of the American Cancer Society, she told me..."

From an interview not performed by you:

Typically include: Name, date, interview source, and credentials

SAY: "Appearing on the television program, *Dateline*, on February 10, 2005, Dr. Michael Beck, a Harvard University economist, argued that..."

From an online magazine:

Typically include: Name of publication, name of reporter and date (providing additional information may give credibility to the source)

SAY: "In his March 17, 2006 column in *Slate*, an online magazine of culture and politics, David Plotz claims that ..."

From a print magazine:

Typically include: Name of publication, name of reporter, and date

SAY: "According to a feature article written by reporter Kelli Brown about the rising costs of medicine in the March 27, 2006 issue of *Time* magazine ..."

From a newspaper:

Typically include: Name of reporter, name of publication, date, and version (i.e. print or electronic version). Providing additional information may give credibility to the source.

SAY: "In a front page article in the January 17, 2006 edition of the *Washington Post* which looked ahead to President Bush's second term, reporter Dana Milbank quoted White House Chief of Staff, Andrew H. Card, Jr., who said, 'President Bush…'"

From a Web log (Blog)

Typically include: Title, name of blogger, website, and date posted

SAY: "National Public Radio reporter Ari Shapiro, in his March 24, 2006 blog titled, "DOJ files voting rights suit," claimed…"

Gratefully used and modified with permission from James Madison University Libraries and the JMU Department of Communication Studies.

SPEAKING ASSIGNMENTS

Introduction Unit
Informative Unit
Persuasive Unit

INTRODUCTION UNIT

The Speech of Introduction

THE SPEECH OF INTRODUCTION

Assignment #1

What Is a Speech of Introduction and Why Is it Required?

"In a Speech of Introduction, you must introduce yourself, another member of your class or someone else in a 2–3 minute time frame by choosing aspects of personal character and experience that are unique, or memorable. Your major responsibility in the introductory speech is to select pertinent information to tell about yourself or someone else so that you or the person you are introducing are **recognized and remembered** as interesting, unique individuals.

Up until this time you may be accustomed to being a "listener" in the classroom situation. In this course, you will be asked also to be a "speaker," which may put you out of your comfort zone as you go forward, turn, and view your audience from a teacher's perspective! You will also be asked to consider your classmates as an "audience," and to discover their unique individual and group characteristics that will help you plan a relevant speech. When you do this, you will begin to discover that public speaking is less about the speaker and more about the "public."

You should select information about your subject based on what you think your audience needs to know about the person you are introducing. The amount of research you do on your subject will depend on whether you are introducing yourself or someone else.

Your audience's general response after hearing your Introduction Speech should be:

■ I am now more familiar with this person.

■ I know this person better. He/she is interesting!

■ I feel more comfortable with this person.

■ This person's nature and character are clearer to me.

In this speech your job is to work hard to achieve these general responses from your audience.

During this speech you also will experience the physical aspects of communicating with an audience (eye contact, volume, rate, articulation, body language). Getting up in front of your classmates right away will help you to adjust to being "on the other side" of the classroom.

Your task is to reveal personal aspects of yourself or someone else to your R110 class (your instructor will give you the precise assignment) in an organized way. Another required task is to listen and make notes about the characteristics of your audience. Hopefully, the facts and insights you will discover about your classmates will help you to become more effective when you prepare later speeches. Also, you will have a better idea of their ages, personalities and interests so you will be able to choose topics that will be beneficial and relevant to their lives.

This speech will help you to adjust to the performance nature of a public speaking class and help you get to know your audience better. (There is only one speech in the Introductory Unit.)

What Skills You Will Learn

1. You will begin to learn how to **select and use creatively pertinent information** about a topic (your "topic" is either you or someone else) which satisfies the purpose of the assignment.

2. You will practice and learn the importance of **displaying appropriate physical behaviors** while communicating orally with an audience (eye contact, volume, rate, articulation, pronunciation, body language, enthusiasm).

3. You will be given the opportunity to **organize ideas and facts** in a logical manner.

4. You will be given the opportunity to experience a **TIMED speaking** activity.

5. You will be given the opportunity to **LISTEN critically** for facts which will help you to characterize the demographics, beliefs, interests, and attitudes of your R110 audience.

What Are the Requirements of this Speech?

1. . . . a **typed or word-processed 3-column outline** with Introduction, Body and Conclusion with appropriate main and sub-points as shown on the sample outline in the following section.

2. . . . that you use no more than **1 note card** (3″ × 5″ or 4″ × 6″, **white index cards**, *not* **paper.**)

3. . . . that you speak a **minimum of 2 and no more than 3 minutes.**

4. . . . OTHER _____

_____

Assignment Tasks: (✔ Check Them Off as You Do Them)

❏ 1. Prepare this assignment using the **Work Sheet** provided. (Be creative!)

❏ 2. On another sheet of paper, prepare an **outline** using the outline format requested.
   ♦ Outline must have an identifiable beginning, middle, and end.

❏ 3. **Type or word-process** your outline. *No exceptions.*

❏ 4. **Rehearse** your speech, using the preparation outline, editing and practicing until it conforms to the time parameters. (minimum, 2 minutes; maximum, 3 minutes)

❏ 5. **Condense the wording in your outline** to key words and phrases and transfer it to 1 note card. Practice with your note card. *DO NOT* write out your speech or preparation outline word-for-word on your note cards!

❏ 6. On the day you speak, hand your **outline and Outline Grading Sheet** to your teacher before you speak along with both copies of the **Speaker Evaluation Sheet.** Deliver your speech from one note card.

❏ 7. **Review your speech on your videotape** and respond to the questions on your **Self-Evaluation Sheet.** Return it to your instructor as per instructor directions.

❏ 8. When you are listening to the speeches of others, make notes on the **Listening Sheet** provided.

> *Keep the Listening Sheet for later use.*

Grading/Evaluative Criteria

Your teacher will evaluate you by using the criteria on the Speaker Evaluation and Outline Grading Sheets that follow the Listening Sheet. He/She will explain the grading system that will be used. Be sure to review the Speaker Evaluation Sheet and Outline Grading Sheet as you prepare for your speech.

Directions

■ Use the outline form on the next page to help organize your thoughts in the speech of introduction. Information asked for is not required, but is strongly suggested for purposes of analyzing audience values, beliefs, attitudes and interests. If you are introducing a person who is not a classmate, such as a historical figure, the organization may change slightly.

■ Please write your introductory/attention-getting statements in complete sentences.

■ Write complete sentences for the main points in the body of your speech.

■ Use complete phrases and clauses for the sub-points.

■ Summarize your thoughts in one or two complete sentences in the conclusion.

■ Use only one idea per symbol.

■ Use the third column on the right to remind yourself of any vocal or physical behaviors you require. (See abbreviated outline following the Speaker Evaluation Sheets and Outline Grading Sheets.)

■ You may add more sub-points to this outline as your time limits permit. Please watch your time carefully!

INTRODUCTION SPEECH: ABBREVIATED 3-COLUMN OUTLINE

Your Name _____ Section _____ Date_____

Purpose: (Who are you introducing?)_____

LEFT COLUMN Label speech function	MIDDLE COLUMN content of speech *Written in Complete Sentences/Phrases*	RIGHT COLUMN Label physical behaviors and delivery cues
	INTRODUCTION	
Attention	I. (Here you should make several interesting statements that will get your audience's attention or that relates you or your subject to your audience or generates curiosity in your topic.)	Remember to speak SLOWLY
Preview	II. (Here you should reveal your topic, *i.e.,* what will the audience know about you/your classmate when you are finished with your speech?)	
	BODY	
Main Point	I. (This category is all personal information)	Remember to speak loudly enough.
Sub Point	A. Name or what subject wants to be called B. Age C. Marital status D. Interesting information about family	
Sub-Sub-Point	1. 2.	
TRANSITION	Transition goes here ("Now that you know a little personal history . . . ")	
Main Point Sub-Point	II. (Educational history goes in this category) A. Describe present education B. Describe educational goals C. Describe current job or career	Remember to LOOK at your audience.
TRANSITION	Transition goes here	

Main Point	III. (Here you should describe the personality—yours or your subject's.)	
Sub-Point	A. Name or describe several things that you LIKE	
Sub-Sub-Point	1.	
	2.	
	3.	
Sub-Point	B. Name or describe several things that you DISLIKE	
Sub-Sub-Point	1.	
	2.	
	3.	
	CONCLUSION	
Signal Conclusion	I. (Include words that indicate you are near the end of your comments: "In conclusion" etc.)	Remember smile and be enthusiastic about your subject!
Summarize	II. (Summarize by indicating what makes you or your subject a unique individual. Repeat your name or the name of the person you are introducing. Make these final comments positive and upbeat about yourself or your subject.)	

INTRODUCTION SPEECH: WORKSHEET

Use this sheet to brainstorm information for your Introduction Speech.

Name of person being introduced (or self): _____

Intriguing aspect of person being introduced:

Life experience: _____

Personality: _____

Beliefs: _____

Goals: _____

Demographic information about person being introduced:

Nickname: _____

Age: _____

Marital status: _____

Education: _____

Likes: _____

Dislikes: _____

Strengths: _____

Weaknesses: _____

Hobbies: _____

Special talents: _____

List several ideas of how you can use the above information to generate interest in your subject: _____

_____

What, from the above information, can you use in an effective introduction? _____

_____

What, from the above information, can you use in an effective conclusion? _____

_____

INTRODUCTION SPEECH: LISTENING SHEET

You may use both sides of this paper to record pertinent information about your R110 classmates. Do not tear this page out of your *Coursebook*.

Demographics: **Number of Audience Members:** _____

Age: 16–20 _____   21–22 _____   23–25 _____   26–30 _____   30+ _____

Gender: Male _____   Female _____

Race: African-American _____   American Indian _____   Asian _____
                     Caucasian _____   Hispanic _____   Other _____

Religion: Agnostic _____   Atheis _____   Buddhist _____
                        Catholic _____   Islamic _____   Protestant _____   Other _____

Marital Status: Married _____   Single _____   Divorced _____
                          Widowed _____   Separated _____   Has children _____

Group Memberships: _____
_____

Remarkable Characteristics: _____
_____

Majors: _____
_____

Hobbies/Interests: _____
_____

Likes: _____
_____

Dislikes: _____
_____

Current jobs: _____
_____

ASSIGNMENT #1

Introduction Speech—Informative

Speaker Evaluation Sheet

I visited the Speaker's Lab for this assignment. Circle one.   YES   NO

Name _____   Section _____   Date _____

Specific Purpose and Central Idea (SP/CI) _____

_____

	Points/Score	Comments

Introduction
- Generated interest in subject   ____/____
- Revealed topic   ____/____

Body
- Utilized 3 main points   ____/____
- Developed main points according to assignment   ____/____

Conclusion
- Prepared audience for ending   ____/____
- Concluded according to Coursebook guidelines   ____/____

Overall
- Maintained time parameters _____   ____/____
- Showed evidence of creativity   ____/____
- Showed evidence of preparation and practice   ____/____

Delivery
- Maintained eye contact with audience   ____/____
- Used effective volume   ____/____
- Used appropriate rate of speaking   ____/____
- Used note card effectively   ____/____
- Displayed enthusiasm   ____/____
- OTHER_____   ____/____

* SPEECH SCORE   ____/____

ASSIGNMENT #1

Introduction Speech—Informative

Assignments & Scores:	
•Speech	_____
Outline	_____
Self-Evaluation	_____

Speaker Evaluation Sheet

I visited the Speaker's Lab for this assignment. Circle one.   **YES**   **NO**

Name _____ Section _____ Date _____

Specific Purpose and Central Idea (SP/CI) _____

_____

                    Points/Score   **Comments**

Introduction
- ◼ Generated interest in subject   ____/____
- ◼ Revealed topic   ____/____

Body
- ◼ Utilized 3 main points   ____/____
- ◼ Developed main points according to assignment   ____/____

Conclusion
- ◼ Prepared audience for ending   ____/____
- ◼ Concluded according to Coursebook guidelines   ____/____

Overall
- ◼ Maintained time parameters _____   ____/____
- ◼ Showed evidence of creativity   ____/____
- ◼ Showed evidence of preparation and practice   ____/____

Delivery
- ◼ Maintained eye contact with audience   ____/____
- ◼ Used effective volume   ____/____
- ◼ Used appropriate rate of speaking   ____/____
- ◼ Used note card effectively   ____/____
- ◼ Displayed enthusiasm   ____/____
- ◼ OTHER_____   ____/____

* SPEECH SCORE   ____/____

ASSIGNMENT #1

Introduction Speech—Informative

Outline Grading Sheet

ATTACH THIS SHEET TO YOUR OUTLINE

Name _____ Section _____ Date _____

Criteria for grading your outline are as follows: Points/Score

Topic/Format
- ▓ Crafted clear Specific Purpose and Central Idea (SP/CI)   _____
- ▓ Used 3-column template—word processed—neat   _____
- ▓ Put delivery cues in third column   _____

Introduction
- ▓ Crafted a 2-part introduction   _____
- ▓ Met minimum requirements for Assignment #1.

Body
- ▓ Crafted 3 main points   _____
- ▓ Developed fully, each point   _____
- ▓ Wrote main and sub-points in complete sentences   _____
- ▓ Stated only ONE idea per symbol.   _____

Conclusion
- ▓ Created 2-part conclusion according to guidelines   _____

Other
- ▓ _____   _____
- ▓ _____   _____

TOTAL OUTLINE SCORE

INTRODUCTION SPEECH: SELF-EVALUATION SHEET

Directions

Review your speech from your video tape. Write a reflective narrative evaluating your performance based on the questions below. Be sure your work is typed or word-processed. See sample self-evaluation(s) in the section following.

- ■ Did I spend enough time gathering information/preparing/practicing? Explain.

- ■ Did I choose interesting information and was I creative with it? Give examples.

- ■ Was my information appropriately organized? Explain.

- ■ Did I make eye contact with the audience?

- ■ Did I use appropriate body language? Give examples.

- ■ Did I use appropriate language and articulation? Was I enthusiastic?

- ■ How did I use my note card? Be specific.

- ■ Did I achieve the time limits? Why or why not?

- ■ What were the things I did well and why were they effective?

- ■ The following things are still in need of correction and here's how I intend to correct them.

THE SPEECH OF INTRODUCTION

NICK POER

Nick Poer
R110—Section No. 7383

Title of Speech—Introduction Speech

Specific Purpose: *To inform my classmates about myself.*

LEFT COLUMN Label speech function	MIDDLE COLUMN content of speech *use complete sentences*	RIGHT COLUMN Label physical behaviors
	INTRODUCTION	
Attention	I. You guys probably remember me as Nick who likes naps. However you won't catch me napping in here, and there's not much to say about naps anyway.	Point quickly to audience Shake head
Reveal Topic	II. That's why today I'm going to tell you a little bit about my personal and educational history, as well as some of my personality.	Point to self
	BODY	(* Fill in any actions, line them up with the appropriate text in the middle column.)

Main Point
Sub-Point
Sub-Sub-Point
	I. Let me begin with some background information.
	  A. First I'll tell you a bit about myself.
	    1. My name is Nick Poer.
	    2. I'm 20 years old.
	    3. I was born here in Indianapolis and have lived here my whole life.
	  B. Now let me talk about my family some.
	    1. I have 3 sisters, all older than me.
	      a. Their names are Melissa, Becca and Krissy.
	      b. Melissa is married and has two kids.
	      c. They are my niece Kaiti and my nephew Quentin.
	      d. Becca lives here in Indy, Krissy lives in Muncie and Melissa lives in Carmel.
	    2. I only have one living grandparent, my maternal grandmother Audrey.
	      a. She is 86 years old.
	      b. Despite having about every non-fatal medical condition imaginable, she continues to persevere.
		Make sure this part sounds funny!

Transition	Since you know me a little better now, I'll tell you about my educational background.	

Main Point
 	
Sub-Point
 	
Sub-Sub-Point
	II. Although I have my struggles like everyone else, I generally consider myself a very good student.
	  A. I graduated just outside the top 10% of my class at North Central High School in 2004.
	    1. I studied Spanish for 6 years from middle school through college, but I hardly consider myself fluent!
	    2. I also played viola, an instrument very similar to the violin, for 5 years in middle school and high school.
	  B. My hard work in high school paid off with an academic scholarship here at IUPUI.
	    1. This is my second year of study at IUPUI and I really enjoy it.
	    2. I'm majoring in Informatics which is a field of IT concerned with using technology to solve problems in non-technological fields such as law, health care administration or geography.
	    3. I have not decided what field of Informatics to branch into but I'm considering New Media and Forensics mainly.
		This should also sound funny!

Transition	Now that you know more about my education, let's talk about things I like and dislike to give you a better sense of who I am.	

Main Point
 	
Sub-Point
 	
Sub-Sub-Point
Sub-Sub-SubPt
	III. For the most part I'm a pretty easy going kind of person just looking to have a good time and enjoy myself whenever I can.
	  A. So first of all I'll tell you about some of the things I like to do.
	    1. I enjoy camping.
	      a. I go twice a year with my family.
	      b. It's a good opportunity to escape the hustle and bustle of life and relax for a few days.
	      c. Some neighbors and friends of the family go camping as well which makes for a very enjoyable time.
	    2. Every Saturday night I go bowling with my sister Becca, her boyfriend Chris and as many of our friends that we can get together.
	    3. I don't watch TV or movies much, but I do enjoy anything with a bit of humor in it.	

	B. As far as things I dislike, there isn't much to talk about.	
	1 My biggest annoyance is anything that causes me stress or boredom, but who likes that stuff, right?	Sarcasm!
	2. I also don't enjoy mornings, I'm definitely not a morning person, sometimes not even an early afternoon person.	Be humorous!
Restate purpose	**CONCLUSION** I. Hopefully now you have gotten to know more about my personal and educational background as well as my personality.	
Clincher/tag/exit line or Final Appeal	II. So if you ever see me around campus looking like I'm about to take a nap, just strike up a conversation about one of the things I told you about myself tonight to keep me awake. Unless it's early in the morning, then I probably need my sleep.	Slight pause

Nick Poer
Introduction Speech Self-Evaluation

I do believe I spent enough time gathering information for, preparing and practicing my introduction speech. Since the speech was about myself there wasn't much time needed to gather information, it was more along the lines of personal reflection and organizing these thoughts into a coherent speech. Once I did that it was pretty easy to prepare and practice my speech which I did 3 times to get the time within the limit.

I do believe I chose interesting information and I was creative with it. I think my attention getter was pretty creative as well as some of the jokes that I put in my speech. I also think my information was interesting because it was more than necessary or expected and that made it unique.

I think my information was appropriately organized because I followed the example in the coursebook and used the 3 column outline provided on the speech lab website.

I did make good eye contact with my audience but towards the end of my speech I started to get a bit more nervous and more reliant on my note card which caused me to make less eye contact than I felt I should have later on.

My body language was appropriate. I used hand gestures well to demonstrate my points however I also seemed to lean on my left foot more than my right foot but I didn't sway or use other inappropriate body language.

I think my language was appropriate for my audience. In my opinion I articulated well with appropriate enthusiasm however I think my enthusiasm seemed to wane as the speech went on.

I used my note card to keep me on track with my speech and to remind me of my attention getter, transitions and clincher. I didn't read off of my note card but I did use it to keep my speech in the order that I outlined it and to remind me of the important things I wanted to say. Towards the end of the speech I needed it more than at the beginning.

Yes I did achieve the time limit; my speech time was approximately 3:05 which is just a little over the time limit but within the 15 second grace period. I practiced my speech 3 times and eliminated information as necessary to make sure that I achieved time limit.

Some of the things I felt I did well were inserting jokes into my speech, my pace was consistent, I followed the outline in the coursebook which gave my speech good organization, I used transitions well and my attention getter and clincher functioned effectively to get my attention's audience and signal the end of my speech. The jokes worked well because they made my speech interesting and they also made me feel less nervous talking to the class. Having a consistent pace was effective so that the class could easily understand what I was saying. Using the coursebook outline examples for my speech was effective because it made my speech well organized and easy to follow. The transitions also helped hold my speech together making them effective.

Among other things I believe I need to work on are body control and posture, being consistent with gestures, and enhancing my enthusiasm. To control my body better I will practice more while trying to keep my body still, possibly standing in a closet so that I have to stand up straight and hold straight. To be more consistent with my gestures I will write my physical cues on my note card with my information as well as practicing those ahead of time with my speech instead of doing them on the fly. And my enthusiasm I can work on by practicing my speeches more and making my speeches as unique and creative as possible.

INFORMATIVE UNIT

Informative Unit Rationale
The Impact Speech
The "What Do You Think?" Speech
The Demonstration Speech
The Speech to Explain

INFORMATIVE UNIT RATIONALE

Why Informative Speeches Are Required

There are endless situations where you will be required to communicate information to others—not in a haphazard, spontaneous way—but in a way that is clear, accurate, meaningful and interesting to the listener. You may need to tell family or friends the exact itinerary of your trip to Europe; you may need to show your replacement how to wrap burritos at Taco Bell; you may be explaining a new benefits package to your colleagues at work. Whatever your situation, you will be constantly telling, showing, or explaining information.

The general audience response after hearing informational speeches (introduction and informational units) should be one of understanding. Understanding is also an audience *expectation* in an informational speech. Your purpose is to craft a speech such that the audience receives a firm mental grasp of the nature, the significance, the character, or the meaning of an idea, a process, a concept, a person, a place, or a thing. Audience response should be "I get it!" or a reaction that indicates that an idea has been made clear and comprehensible. Therefore, in this unit you will be required to prepare two informative speeches.

The Impact Speech and The "What Do You Think?" Speech are informative speeches that will give you an opportunity to practice adapting your thoughts and material to your audience in an organized way. The Speech to Demonstrate involves showing and telling how something is done, made, works, or is fixed. It is an informative speech with a visual, procedural focus. Your audience should know how to perform this task when you have finished with your speech. Your teacher will assign you ONE of these speeches.

In the Speech to Explain a concept, event, process, or object, you will be communicating information so that your audience will understand thoroughly the information you have shared. This speech is given after the one above and is required of ALL students.

Skills you will learn and exact requirements for each speech follow.

THE IMPACT SPEECH

Assignment #2

What Is the Impact Speech and Why Is it required?

The Impact Speech, which is an informative-type speech, will give you experience sharing with others the impact a person, place, thing or event has had on you. You will also be asked to share how your experience relates to the lives of your audience. You will share this person, place, thing or event with your audience in three ways (**these will be your three main points**):

1. You will give a **history** of the person, place, thing, or event.

2. You will tell how that person, place, thing or event has made **its impact on you** personally, and

3. You will share with your audience how that person, place, thing, or event offers beneficial "life lessons" to your audience.

How Will You Benefit from Doing a Speech of this Type?

Although you will understand very well why your choice of subject is important to you, your audience will not necessarily understand why it is important to them. **This speech gives you the opportunity to think about the various ways you can make a topic relevant to an audience.** Hopefully the skills you will learn in this speech will transfer to your subsequent speeches thus making them more relevant, enjoyable and beneficial to your audience.

The general audience response you should work for should include the following:

■ This person, place, or thing is really important to the speaker.

■ I understand more completely the value this speaker puts on this person, place, or thing.

■ This person, place or thing has relevance to me, too!

■ I have learned something from the speaker's experience with this person, place or thing.

What Skills You Will Learn

1. You will learn how to **select a topic** that will be beneficial to your audience.

2. You will **construct a narrow specific purpose and central idea** to guide your speech.

3. You will learn to use a **simple 3-point topical organizational structure.**

4. You will **develop each main point with your audience's interest** and benefit in mind.

5. You will **practice using an audio-visual aid** to support and enhance your "choice."

6. You will **practice using descriptive language.**

7. You will practice extemporaneous delivery skills (use of note cards, eye contact, body language, volume, rate, articulation, etc.)

Sample Topics

1. How the computer has influenced my life.

2. Stephen Hawking is my role model.

3. How the military shaped my character.

4. How becoming a parent is the most important thing in my life.

5. The Coliseum in Rome is my favorite place.

What Are the Requirements for this Speech?

1. A **beneficial topic for your audience**

2. A **clear, narrow specific purpose** and **central idea** statement containing the three main points (see description of speech—previous page)

3. A **typed or word-processed 3-column preparation outline** with the following functions labeled:

    ■ *introduction and parts*

    ■ *body and parts (three main points)*

    ■ *conclusion and parts*

    ■ *transitions between main points written out*

    ■ *physical behaviors indicated in right column*

4. One outside source (other than yourself)

5. **One audio-visual aid,** minimum

6. **2 note cards,** maximum, turned in after your speech

7. **Time limit:** 5 minutes minimum, 7 minutes maximum

8. Completed **Audience Analysis/ Adaptation Sheet**

9. **Required self-evaluation** submitted to instructor as directed

10. Other _____

Task Checklist (✔ check off as you complete each task)

❏ 1. Using your Listening Sheet and your completed Audience Analysis from the Introduction Speech, **choose a subject** that has potential interest and relevance to your classroom audience.

❏ 2. Construct your **specific purpose** and **central idea** with your audience in mind.

❏ 3. Create your **preparation outline,** making sure you give equal development to all three main points.

❏ 4. **Choose/Create your visual(s):** Ask yourself:

    ■ What will help the audience visually or aurally to understand how important this person, place, thing, or event is to me?

    ■ What or how much do I have to show the audience to make this subject interesting and relevant to them?

    ■ Save your visuals to RESOURCES in Oncourse CL. Bring visuals to class on a flash drive or CDROM.

❏ 5. **Practice** with your preparation outline. **Time** yourself. **Edit** material if necessary.

❏ 6. **Create your note cards. Practice** with cards and visual(s). **Time** yourself. **Edit** if necessary. *DO NOT write out your speech or preparation outline word-for-word on your note cards!*

❏ 7. **Assess the room situation** and come prepared to arrange or set up audio-visual aids.

❏ 8. Give your instructor your preparation outline with **Outline Grading Sheet** attached, the audience analysis, and both **Speaker Evaluation Sheets** before you speak.

❏ 9. After your speech, **view your videotape.** Thoughtfully write your **Self-Evaluation essay** and submit to your instructor by deadline.

Grading Criteria

Grading Criteria for this Speech: See the Speaker Evaluation form and the Outline Grading Sheet in the Coursebook. *Apply these criteria to what you have prepared in order to optimize your grade points.*

IMPACT SPEECH
AUDIENCE ANALYSIS/ADAPTATION SHEET

Directions

Study the Listening Sheet you completed from the Introduction Speech. Based on the information you gathered by listening to the Introduction Speeches of your classmates and informal observations you may have made, answer the following questions: (TYPE OR WORD-PROCESS YOUR ANSWERS AND ESSAY ON A SEPARATE SHEET. Submit per teacher instructions.)

Demographic Audience Information

1. What is the average age of your audience? What is the age range?

2. How many males in your class? Females?

3. Are there any non-native speakers? If so, how many and from where?

4. How many of your classmates are married? How many have children?

5. Can you name 2 or 3 things that the majority of your classmates have in common?

6. If a friend asked you to describe your classmates in R110, how would you describe them as a group?

Adaptation

7. In essay form tell why you think that this topic may be important to your audience (cite any relevant attitudes, beliefs, demographic or situational characteristics to back up your thoughts.) Also, as you look over your answers to the questions above, how can you use this information to craft a speech that is relevant/beneficial/interesting to your classmates?"

ASSIGNMENT #2

Impact Speech—Informative

Assignments & Scores:
- Speech _____
- Outline _____
- Audience Analysis _____
- Self-Evaluation _____

Speaker Evaluation Sheet

I visited the Speaker's Lab for this assignment. Circle one.   YES   NO

Name _____ Section _____ Date _____

Specific Purpose and Central Idea (SP/CI) _____

_____

	Points/Score	Comments

Introduction
- ■ Gained attention/interest ____/____
- ■ Revealed topic clearly (SP) ____/____
- ■ Showed relevance to audience ____/____
- ■ Established speaker credibility ____/____
- ■ Previewed body of speech (CI) ____/____

Body
- ■ Three main points organized & presented clearly ____/____
- ■ Main points fully developed ____/____
- ■ Transitions effectively presented ____/____
- ■ Clearly described benefits to audience ____/____
- ■ Chose descriptive language ____/____

Conclusion
- ■ Audience prepared for conclusion ____/____
- ■ Purpose or points reviewed or summarized ____/____

Delivery
- ■ Used extemporaneous delivery style ____/____
- ■ Maintained eye contact ____/____
- ■ Used voice effectively ____/____
  (vol., rate, pitch, artic., voc. pauses, etc.)
- ■ Used body/gestures/space effectively ____/____
- ■ Used note cards effectively ____/____
- ■ Showed enthusiasm ____/____
- ■ Evidence of preparation and practice ____/____

Overall
- ■ Maintained time parameters _____ ____/____
- ■ Effective selection, preparation and use
  of visual aid ____/____
- ■ Sources effectively cited (1 source minimum) ____/____

* SPEECH SCORE ____/____

ASSIGNMENT #2

Impact Speech—Informative

Speaker Evaluation Sheet

I visited the Speaker's Lab for this assignment. Circle one.   YES   NO

Name _____ Section _____ Date _____

Specific Purpose and Central Idea (SP/CI) _____

_____

	Points/Score	Comments

Introduction
- Gained attention/interest   ____/____
- Revealed topic clearly (SP)   ____/____
- Showed relevance to audience   ____/____
- Established speaker credibility   ____/____
- Previewed body of speech (CI)   ____/____

Body
- Three main points organized & presented clearly ____/____
- Main points fully developed   ____/____
- Transitions effectively presented   ____/____
- Clearly described benefits to audience   ____/____
- Chose descriptive language   ____/____

Conclusion
- Audience prepared for conclusion   ____/____
- Purpose or points reviewed or summarized   ____/____

Delivery
- Used extemporaneous delivery style   ____/____
- Maintained eye contact   ____/____
- Used voice effectively   ____/____
  (vol., rate, pitch, artic., voc. pauses, etc.)
- Used body/gestures/space effectively   ____/____
- Used note cards effectively   ____/____
- Showed enthusiasm   ____/____
- Evidence of preparation and practice   ____/____

Overall
- Maintained time parameters _____   ____/____
- Effective selection, preparation and use
  of visual aid   ____/____
- Sources effectively cited (1 source minimum)   ____/____

* SPEECH SCORE   ____/____

ASSIGNMENT #2

Impact Speech—Informative

Outline Grading Sheet

ATTACH THIS SHEET TO YOUR OUTLINE

Name _____ **Section** _____ **Date** _____

Criteria for grading your outline are as follows:　　　　　　**Points/Score**

Topic/Format

- Chose subject appropriate to assignment　　　　　　_____
- Wrote clear and narrow specific purpose and central idea　_____
- Used 3-column outline template　　　　　　　　　　_____
- Wrote main and sub-points in complete sentences, word-processed　_____
- Proper coordination, subordination, symbolization, indentation　_____

Introduction—labeled

- Effectively crafted and labeled all 5 parts of introduction　_____

Body—labeled

- Created 3 main points according to requirements—labeled　_____
- Developed each point fully, balanced　　　　　　　_____
- Wrote out transitions in complete sentences—labeled　_____
- Stated one idea per symbol　　　　　　　　　　　_____

Conclusion—labeled

- Crafted 2-part conclusion and labeled parts　　　　_____

Over-all

- Noted delivery or visual cues in 3rd column　　　　_____
- Used proper in-text citation (one source minimum)　_____
- Proper Works Cited page (MLA)　　　　　　　　　_____
- Note cards (Key Word Outline) reflects preparation outline　_____

TOTAL OUTLINE SCORE　　　　　　　　　　　_____

Impact Speech: Peer Listening Sheet (1)

Speaker _____   Listener _____

Section# _____   Topic _____

A. Audience Adaptation

1. How did this speaker adapt this speech to you?

2. How could this speaker better adapt this speech to you and the rest of the audience?

B. Delivery

1. What were the two strongest aspects of delivery used by this speaker (example: eye contact, volume, rate, articulation, enthusiasm/sincerity, body language etc.?).

2. Name one aspect of delivery the speaker should work on before the next speech.

C. Clarity of language and message

1. What are two ways this speaker made the message memorable enough so that you could tell it to someone else? (example: specific language use, transitions, organization, the audio-visual aids, etc.)

2. How could this speaker make the message clearer to you?

IMPACT SPEECH: PEER LISTENING SHEET (2)

Speaker _____   Listener _____

Section# _____   Topic _____

A. Audience Adaptation

1. How did this speaker adapt this speech to you?

2. How could this speaker better adapt this speech to you and the rest of the audience?

B. Delivery

1. What were the two strongest aspects of delivery used by this speaker (example: eye contact, volume, rate, articulation, enthusiasm/sincerity, body language etc.?).

2. Name one aspect of delivery the speaker should work on before the next speech.

C. Clarity of language and message

1. What are two ways this speaker made the message memorable enough so that you could tell it to someone else? (example: specific language use, transitions, organization, the audio-visual aids, etc.)

2. How could this speaker make the message clearer to you?

Impact Speech:
Peer Listening Sheet (3)

Speaker _____ Listener _____

Section# _____ Topic _____

A. Audience Adaptation

1. How did this speaker adapt this speech to you?

2. How could this speaker better adapt this speech to you and the rest of the audience?

B. Delivery

1. What were the two strongest aspects of delivery used by this speaker (example: eye contact, volume, rate, articulation, enthusiasm/sincerity, body language etc.?).

2. Name one aspect of delivery the speaker should work on before the next speech.

C. Clarity of language and message

1. What are two ways this speaker made the message memorable enough so that you could tell it to someone else? (example: specific language use, transitions, organization, the audio-visual aids, etc.)

2. How could this speaker make the message clearer to you?

IMPACT SPEECH:
PEER LISTENING SHEET (4)

Speaker _____ Listener _____

Section# _____ Topic _____

A. Audience Adaptation

1. How did this speaker adapt this speech to you?

2. How could this speaker better adapt this speech to you and the rest of the audience?

B. Delivery

1. What were the two strongest aspects of delivery used by this speaker (example: eye contact, volume, rate, articulation, enthusiasm/sincerity, body language etc.?).

2. Name one aspect of delivery the speaker should work on before the next speech.

C. Clarity of language and message

1. What are two ways this speaker made the message memorable enough so that you could tell it to someone else? (example: specific language use, transitions, organization, the audio-visual aids, etc.)

2. How could this speaker make the message clearer to you?

IMPACT SPEECH:
PEER LISTENING SHEET (5)

Speaker _____ Listener _____

Section# _____ Topic _____

A. Audience Adaptation

1. How did this speaker adapt this speech to you?

2. How could this speaker better adapt this speech to you and the rest of the audience?

B. Delivery

1. What were the two strongest aspects of delivery used by this speaker (example: eye contact, volume, rate, articulation, enthusiasm/sincerity, body language etc.?).

2. Name one aspect of delivery the speaker should work on before the next speech.

C. Clarity of language and message

1. What are two ways this speaker made the message memorable enough so that you could tell it to someone else? (example: specific language use, transitions, organization, the audio-visual aids, etc.)

2. How could this speaker make the message clearer to you?

Impact Speech: Peer Listening Sheet (6)

Speaker _____   Listener _____

Section# _____   Topic _____

A. Audience Adaptation

1. How did this speaker adapt this speech to you?

2. How could this speaker better adapt this speech to you and the rest of the audience?

B. Delivery

1. What were the two strongest aspects of delivery used by this speaker (example: eye contact, volume, rate, articulation, enthusiasm/sincerity, body language etc.?).

2. Name one aspect of delivery the speaker should work on before the next speech.

C. Clarity of language and message

1. What are two ways this speaker made the message memorable enough so that you could tell it to someone else? (example: specific language use, transitions, organization, the audio-visual aids, etc.)

2. How could this speaker make the message clearer to you?

IMPACT SPEECH:
PEER LISTENING SHEET (7)

Speaker _____ Listener _____

Section# _____ Topic _____

A. Audience Adaptation

1. How did this speaker adapt this speech to you?

2. How could this speaker better adapt this speech to you and the rest of the audience?

B. Delivery

1. What were the two strongest aspects of delivery used by this speaker (example: eye contact, volume, rate, articulation, enthusiasm/sincerity, body language etc.?).

2. Name one aspect of delivery the speaker should work on before the next speech.

C. Clarity of language and message

1. What are two ways this speaker made the message memorable enough so that you could tell it to someone else? (example: specific language use, transitions, organization, the audio-visual aids, etc.)

2. How could this speaker make the message clearer to you?

IMPACT SPEECH: SELF-EVALUATION SHEET

Directions

Review your speech from your video tape. Write a **reflective narrative** evaluating your performance and basing your comments on your thoughtful responses to the concerns and issues below. Be sure your work is typed or word-processed. Submit per instructor's directions. See sample impact self-evaluation in the section following.

- Did I spend enough time gathering information and preparing/practicing? Explain.

- Did I use my audio/visual aid(s) effectively? Why or why not?

- Was my information appropriately organized? Explain.

- How did I adapt this speech to my audience?

- Did I make effective eye contact with the audience?

- Did I use appropriate body language? Give examples.

- Was I understandable and enthusiastic?

- Did I achieve the time limits, why or why not?

- How did I use my note cards? Explain.

- What parts of my speech were most effective? Be specific and tell why. Cite evidence from Peer Evaluations as well as teacher response from Speaker Evaluation.

- What things were least effective? Be specific and tell why. Cite evidence from Peer Evaluations as well as teacher response from Speaker Evaluation.

- How did I adapt this speech to my audience? Cite evidence from Peer Evaluations as well as teacher response from Speaker Evaluation.

- What specific things am I going to improve upon for the next speech and how? List each improvement desired and how you will accomplish it.

THE IMPACT SPEECH

S
A
M
P
L
E

LAURA BIEHL

SAMPLE IMPACT SPEECH
AUDIENCE ANALYSIS—LAURA BIEHL

1. **What is the average age of your audience? What is the age range?**

    There are the same number of students who are 21–22 as there are students over 30.

    There are four students under 21, and there are students who are between 23 and 30, so we have a very wide range of ages.

2. **How many males in your class? Females?**

    There are 13 females and 9 males in our class.

3. **Are there any non-native speakers? If so, how many and from where?**

    There are no non-native speakers.

4. **How many of your classmates are married? How many have children?**

    Five people are married (a few more are engaged), and 9 have children.

5. **Can you name 2 or 3 things that the majority of your classmates have in common?**

    Most of us seem to be working on our first degree. A large majority is Caucasian.

    Most of our majors, although not directly connected with making speeches, are going towards careers where communication with others is important.

6. **If a friend asked you to describe your classmates in R110, how would you describe them as a group?**

    Even though we have an incredible amount of differences, we have a lot of similarities that bring us together. We care about our education, we are devoted to our families, and we want to be treated well by others. For the large part, we aren't expert speech-makers, but I can see strengths in each person's style, and I think we all want to learn how to be better.

7. **How are you planning to use any of your audience's demographic or attitudinal characteristics to help you choose a subject and/or prepare a speech which they can really relate to? Be specific and write in essay form below. (This is the most important part. It should relate directly to your third main point.)**

    Because I am planning on being an elementary school teacher, I have strong feelings about the necessity of getting children to read. It is a belief that I would like to share with as many as possible, and given the age demographics of my audience, I felt like this was an appropriate place to do so. At least nine people have children right now, and a large number are either married or engaged. It is highly likely that most everyone in our class will have children that they can influence, and perhaps my speech will cause them to want to include reading as an activity. I learned in a human development class that the best time to teach a person something is either right when it is happening or when it is in the near future. For most of our class, now seems to be a time when children are in the foreground of their minds.

Laura Biehl

R110—Impact Speech Preparation Outline

Title of Speech—(optional)

Specific Purpose: To inform my audience of how the television show *Reading Rainbow* influenced my appreciation for reading.

Central Idea: *Reading Rainbow* has been teaching children the importance of reading for almost twenty years, has helped instill a love for reading in myself, and can open the world of books to your children and grandchildren now and in the future.

LEFT COLUMN Label speech function	MIDDLE COLUMN Content of speech *Written in Complete* *Sentences/Phrases*	RIGHT COLUMN Label physical behaviors and delivery cues
	INTRODUCTION	
Attention	I. My knowledge of the importance of reading did not come from college courses—it came from LeVar Burton and *Reading Rainbow* on PBS	Look at audience
Reveal Topic	II. *Reading Rainbow* helped develop my love of reading.	
Relevancy	III. Most of us will either be parents or have the opportunity to influence a child, and it is necessary to encourage reading	
Credibility	IV. As a future schoolteacher, I have learned the importance of reading.	
Preview	V. I will talk about *Reading Rainbow,* how the show affected me, and how it can help the children in your life.	Play tape
	BODY	
Main Point	I. *Reading Rainbow* has been sharing the joys of literature with children since 1983 in a way that is unique to the program. (Wood, Duke 96)	
Sub-Point	A. Each show is divided into sections to share information.	
Sub-Sub-Point	1. One book is chosen as the focus, and all of the activities revolve around that book in some way.	
	2. In the show based on the book *Sam the Sea Cow,* all of the segments focus on manatees and endangered animals. (Liggett 37)	
	B. We all have different styles of learning, and the segments on *Reading Rainbow* reflect those differences.	
	1. Harvard Professor Howard Gardner identified eight ways of learning, including musically, logically, and through movement. (Gardner 4)	

	2. *Reading Rainbow* has used songs, art projects, dance numbers, and many other approaches to cover the different ways of learning. (Wood, Duke 97)	
TRANSITION	Now that you know a little more of what *Reading Rainbow* is about, I want to share my personal experience with it.	
Main Point	II. *Reading Rainbow* had a great impact on my love for reading.	Keep volume up
Sub-Point Sub-Sub-Point	A. I learned to see the world in a different way. 1. When I started reading on my own, I realized how many things there were that I wanted to learn about. 2. The subjects I learned about on *Reading Rainbow* fascinated me, and many questions I had about the world were answered. B. I felt I could relate to the people on the show. 1. Now only was there a good adult role model, but there were also peers my own age who were describing how much they loved to read. 2. I practiced giving my own book talks.	
TRANSITION	While you can probably see how *Reading Rainbow* is helpful, you may wonder how this is useful in your lives.	
Main Point	III. *Reading Rainbow* can be an excellent tool to open the joy of books to all children in your life.	
Sub-Point	A. In a world focused on television and computers, it is important that we encourage reading.	
Sub-Sub-Point	1. Laura Bush, a former librarian as well as the First Lady, has made it clear that she and the President feel reading is important. (US News 11) 2. It is necessary for us role models to teach children good reading habits.	
Sub-Point	B. *Reading Rainbow* helps children in at least two essential ways. 1. It introduces children to quality literature. 2. It promotes personal discovery of other literature.	
Sub-Sub-Sub-Point	a. 82% of librarians say children "ask for books they saw on the program." (Wood, Duke 96) b. I can remember on episode specifically that influenced me to find out more on my own.	

Restate purpose (review of Main Points)	**CONCLUSION**	
I. Through the years *Reading Rainbow* has been an inspiration to many children, including me, as an example of how reading can be fun. It will likely continue in the future as a beacon to all.	
Clincher/tag/exit line	II. Natalie Babbitt, a children's author, said, "Reading should be a joy . . . not a responsibility, not something you do because society demand it, but something you do because it's a pleasure." (Babbitt 141)	Look at audience —Smile

Works Cited

Babbitt, N. (2000). *Tuck Everlasting* (3rd ed.). United States of America: Sunburst. [Interview by Betsy Hearne (pp. 141–171)].

Gardner, Howard. "Howard Gardner on Making the Most of Young Minds." *Education Digest,* Feb 2000, Vol. 65, Issue 6, p. 4, 3p.

Kulman, L. & Silver, M. (2001, September 10). Passionate about turning pages. *U.S. News & World Report, 131*(9), p. 11.

Liggett, T.C. & Benfield, C.M. (1996). *Reading Rainbow guide to children's books: the 101 best titles.* Secaucus, N.J. : Carol Publishing Group.

Wood, J. M. & Duke, N. K. (1997, February). "Inside 'Reading Rainbow': A spectrum of strategies for promoting literacy." *Language Arts,* Feb. 97, Vol. 74, Issue 2, p. 95, 12p.

Impact Speech Self-Evaluation—Laura Biehl

This was quite the learning experience. I have probably given twenty or more speeches in my life, but this was the first time I have actually been in a speech class, and I also teach once a month at my church, but I soon realized that a speech and a lesson have quite different styles. There were some things I did right, and some things I did wrong, and definitely some things I can work on.

Since I tend to be critical of myself, I had a harder time finding what I did right. I still like my video clip that I used. I thought it was different from the other visual aids, and every time I hear that song, it transports me back in time, and I am sure it did the same for anyone who used to watch the show. Second, I was more comfortable when I talked about my own experience, and I did become a little more relaxed once I got into that section. I did not have a lot of distracting mannerisms (which is something I am famous for, so I am proud of myself for cutting those out), and I tried not to move around a lot. I also did an okay job of keeping good eye contact. I also thought I had a good quote for the conclusion that summed up how I felt.

Where do I begin with what I did wrong? First I spoke way too fast. I knew I was doing that as I spoke, and I cringed hearing myself on tape. Part of the problem was I had timed myself beforehand, and I knew my speech was a little longer than it should be, so I think I subconsciously decided to speak faster to cram everything in. It was not a good idea, especially since I normally have a problem speaking slowly. I also need to project. Being a quiet person, this concept is hard for me, but the things I have to say are important, so I need to make sure everyone can hear. I also really messed up my introduction because I got nervous. My nervousness also caused me to say, "Umm and kinda" a lot, which I know detracts from a speech. I also looked at my cards an awful lot. I could tell where I gave examples that were not on my cards because that was when I looked at the audience the whole time I was speaking.

Most of the things I did wrong are the things I can work on. I will cut out any excess information if I know my speech will be too long. That way I will not try to cram it all in. I will also make sure that I practice pauses. I tend to worry that I will lose my train of thought if I do not keep going, but it sure cuts out on my enthusiasm if I am thinking about the next point before I am done with the one I am on. Projection may be a problem, but I also noticed that I spoke at about the same level I practiced at. Next time I will practice as if I have to be heard in a large room instead of just to be heard by myself. The hardest thing will be writing less on my note cards. I have heard a thousand times that I do not need everything written down, and I knew that speech well enough that I should not have been looking at my cards, but the fact that what I wanted to say was written down extensively caused me to look at my cards much too often. I did not even realize how much I had looked down until I watched the video. For the next speech I will write down less, even if it does scare me. But I have never tried having just keywords, so now is the time to prove to myself that I can do it. I am *very* excited about the next speech, and I want to do well, so I plan on working hard to correct these things and make the experience enjoyable for the audience, as well as for myself.

The "What Do *You* Think?" Speech

What is the "What Do *You* Think?" Speech?

Every day of our lives, we are asked by others to articulate our ideas. "What do you think?" is a question commonly asked in informal conversations and in formal settings like class or the workplace. Being able to speak your thoughts clearly and accurately is an important skill needed by everyone. This speaking assignment is designed to give you practice in stating your opinions, thoughts, and insights. In the "What Do *You* Think?" Speech, you are asked to choose an aspect of the assigned movie that has made a significant impact upon you. You will organize your thoughts utilizing these three main points:

1. You will describe, in detail, the part(s) of the movie that inspired your thoughts (your main point I.)

2. You will tell how that idea or event from the movie has made its impact on you personally, (your main point II.) and

3. You will share with your audience how this idea or event could possibly make a difference in the lives of your audience (your main point III.)

Why you will benefit from doing a speech of this type.

You will benefit from this assignment because you will be given the opportunity to develop and share your own thoughts with others. The movie _____, is this semester's required viewing. You may have seen this movie already. You may or may not have liked or enjoyed it. No matter. Look for an idea, a thought or a personal lesson from this film that you can develop in an interesting way. Remember that the point is to TELL WHAT YOU THINK. These are your thoughts and they are not "right or wrong." They represent your thoughtful and insightful reflections on an idea or event that comes from this film. If you are one of the people who honestly did not care for the film the first time you saw it, when you see it again, approach your viewing with this speech purpose in mind. If you are still unsure of what idea or theme to develop, search for the movie website or the online movie chat room or a movie review or blog, and check out what others might be saying about the film and what they learned from it or liked about it. Note: THIS SPEECH IS **NOT** A MOVIE REVIEW!

The audience expectation and response after you give your speech should include the following reactions:

1. This is a fascinating idea/reaction from the movie.

2. This idea from the movie has had a really significant impact on the speaker.

3. This idea actually has relevance to me.

4. I have learned something from this speaker's reaction to this idea.

What skills you will learn

1. You will learn how to select a topic that will be beneficial /of interest to your audience.

2. You will construct a narrow specific purpose and central idea to guide your speech.

3. You will learn to use a simple 3-main point organizational structure (See What is the "What Do *You* Think?"Speech, 1.2.3 above).

4. You will develop three main points with your audience's interests in mind.

5. You will practice using an audio-visual aid to support and illustrate your ideas.

6. You will practice using descriptive language.

7. You will practice extemporaneous delivery skills (use of note cards, eye contact, body language, volume, rate, articulation, etc.)

SUGGESTIONS FOR BEGINNING THE ASSIGNMENT

* Rent the movie and view it. If you have already seen it, watch it again.

* If you are affected in some positive way by something that happens in the film, or an idea that occurs to you because of something that the film deals with, mentally note that place in the film. This will help your audience to understand the impact the movie had on you. Then....

* Try to articulate, in one sentence, the idea that impressed you. Keep writing until you can get this into one sentence.

* Fashion your idea into a Specific Purpose sentence that will start out like this:" To tell or explain how XYZ idea from the movie has impacted me." (See examples in next section.)

* Then, make your Central Idea according to the three points above: (See textbook, Chapter 4 about how to phrase a Central idea. Your central idea should contain, or strongly hint at the three points above (description, personal impact, audience impact).

* The three points alluded to in your Central Idea will be the three main points of your outline. This will help you organize the flow of your ideas and will create the superstructure for your outline.

* Your visual aid should be something that illustrates your idea literally or symbolically. For example, it could be a picture from the movie, or an object that symbolically represents what idea you are dealing with in the movie. The visual can take any form and is not weighed heavily in this speech. Use a simple visual to create audience interest, for clarification, or to increase retention of information.

Sample Specific Purposes and Central Ideas from students who viewed "Napoleon Dynamite."

1. **Specific Purpose:** To inform the audience how the idea of friendship from Napoleon Dynamite has impacted me.

   Central Idea: The friendship between Napoleon and Pedro is highlighted in three scenes of the movie, has given me a different perspective on the idea of friendship, and can cause you to become more appreciative of your own friendships.

2. **Specific purpose:** To explain how the issue of "living in the past" as manifested in Napoleon Dynamite has impacted me.

   Central idea: In Napoleon Dynamite, Uncle Rico lives in the past, and this has shown me how important it is to live in the present and not dwell on "what might have been," - an important lesson for everyone!

Here are the Requirements for This Speech.

1. **Discover an interesting idea** inspired by the movie that you can share with your audience.

2. **Write a clear, narrow specific purpose and central idea** statement to guide the flow of your thoughts.

3. **Create your 3 main points,** using the 3 points under "What is the "What Do *You* Think? Speech", above.

4. **Prepare an outline,** using the 3-column template and the template explanation with the following functions labeled: (See sample Impact outline link below)

   * Introduction and parts

   * Body and parts

   * Conclusion and parts

   * Transitions between main points written out at appropriate places in outline and labeled

   * Physical behaviors describe in the right column

5. **Orally cite one outside source** ("According to....") and document it on a Works Cited page and within the outline (see in-text source citations in the MLA section of this book.)

6. **Use one audio-visual aid,** minimum

7. **Use 2 note cards,** maximum, turned in after your speech

8. **Achieve time limit:** 5 minutes minimum and 7 minutes maximum.

9. Hand in **completed Audience Analysis** Sheet before you give your speech as directed by your instructor.

10. **Submit self-evaluation** as directed by your instructor.

11. Bring a brand new, VHS **videotape of high quality** to your speech class. You may not speak without it.

Checklist to help you prepare your speech.

❏ 1. Using the Listening Sheet and Audience Analysis from your last assignment, think about how your ideas have potential interest and relevance to your classroom audience.

❏ 2. **Construct your specific purpose and central idea** with your audience in mind.

❏ 3. **Create your preparation outline,** making sure you give balanced development to all three points (description, personal impact, audience impact).

❏ 4. **Choose/create your visual(s);** Ask yourself:

   ▪ What audio or visual aid will help my audience to engage with my idea(s) from the movie?

   ▪ What or how much do I have to show the audience to make this subject interesting and relevant to them?

   ▪ Save your visuals to RESOURCES in Oncourse CL. Bring visuals to class on a flash drive or CDROM

❏ 5. **Practice with your preparation outline.** Time yourself. Edit material if necessary.

❏ 6. **Create your key word outline on note cards.** Practice with cards and visual(s). Edit material if necessary, and use key words/phrases to remind you what to say. *DO NOT write out your speech or preparation outline word-for-word on your note cards!*

❏ 7. **Assess room situation.** Do you know anything about the equipment in your classroom? How can you find out? What kind of equipment will you need? Come prepared to arrange or set up your visuals, etc.

❏ 8. **Hand your instructor your preparation outline with Outline Grading Sheet attached, and both copies of the Speaker Evaluation form.** Fill out the top portions of the forms before you submit them to your instructor in a double-pocketed folder.

❏ 9. Grading will be based on the Speaker Evaluation Sheet and Outline Grading Sheet included with your printed Coursebook materials.

❏ 10. After you give your speech in class, **return home and view your videotaped speech.** Thoughtfully write your Self-evaluation and submit to your instructor as directed. Use your instructor's comments and peer review sheets to help you write your self-evaluation.

Grading Criteria for this Speech: See the Speaker Evaluation form and the Outline Grading Sheet in the Coursebook. *Apply the criteria to what you have prepared to optimize your grade points.*

"WHAT DO *YOU* THINK?" SPEECH: AUDIENCE ANALYSIS/ADAPTATION SHEET

Directions:

Study the Listening Sheet you completed from the Introduction Speech. Based on the information you gathered by listening to the Introduction Speeches of your classmates and informal observations you may have made, answer the following questions: (**TYPE OR WORD-PROCESS YOUR ANSWERS AND ESSAY ON A SEPARATE SHEET.** Submit per instructor's directions.)

Demographic Audience Information

1. What is the average age of your audience? What is the age range

2. How many males in your class? Females?

3. Are there any non-native speakers? If so, how many and from where?

4. How many of your classmates are married? How many have children

5. Can you name 2 or 3 things that the majority of your classmates have in common?

6. If a friend asked you to describe your classmates in R110, how would you describe them as a group?

Adaptation

7. In essay form tell why you think that this topic may be important to your audience (cite any relevant attitudes, beliefs, demographic or situational characteristics to back up your thoughts.) Also, as you look over your answers to the questions above, how can you use this information to craft a speech that is relevant/beneficial/interesting to your classmates?

ASSIGNMENT #3

"What Do *You* Think?"—Informative

Speaker Evaluation Sheet

I visited the Speaker's Lab for this assignment. Circle one.   YES   NO

Name _____ Section _____ Date _____

Specific Purpose and Central Idea (SP/CI) _____

_____

	Points/Score	Comments

Introduction

- Gained attention/interest   ____/____
- Revealed topic clearly (SP)   ____/____
- Showed relevance to audience   ____/____
- Established speaker credibility   ____/____
- Previewed body of speech (CI)   ____/____

Body

- Three main points presented clearly   ____/____
- Main points fully developed   ____/____
- Transitions effectively presented   ____/____
- Source effectively cited   ____/____
- Chose descriptive language   ____/____

Conclusion

- Audience prepared for conclusion   ____/____
- Purpose or points reviewed or summarized   ____/____

Delivery

- Used extemporaneous delivery style   ____/____
- Maintained eye contact   ____/____
- Used voice effectively   ____/____
  (vol., rate, pitch, artic., voc. pauses, etc.)
- Used body /gestures /space effectively   ____/____
- Used note cards effectively   ____/____
- Showed enthusiasm   ____/____
- Evidence of preparation and practice   ____/____

Overall

- Maintained time parameters _____   ____/____
- Effective selection, preparation and use of visual aid   ____/____
- Personal involvement evident   ____/____

* SPEECH SCORE   ____/____

ASSIGNMENT #3

"What Do *You* Think?"—Informative

Speaker Evaluation Sheet

I visited the Speaker's Lab for this assignment. Circle one.   YES   NO

Name _____   Section _____   Date _____

Specific Purpose and Central Idea (SP/CI) _____

_____

	Points/Score	Comments
Introduction		
■ Gained attention/interest	____/____	
■ Revealed topic clearly (SP)	____/____	
■ Showed relevance to audience	____/____	
■ Established speaker credibility	____/____	
■ Previewed body of speech (CI)	____/____	
Body		
■ Three main points presented clearly	____/____	
■ Main points fully developed	____/____	
■ Transitions effectively presented	____/____	
■ Source effectively cited	____/____	
■ Chose descriptive language	____/____	
Conclusion		
■ Audience prepared for conclusion	____/____	
■ Purpose or points reviewed or summarized	____/____	
Delivery		
■ Used extemporaneous delivery style	____/____	
■ Maintained eye contact	____/____	
■ Used voice effectively	____/____	
(vol., rate, pitch, artic., voc. pauses, etc.)		
■ Used body /gestures /space effectively	____/____	
■ Used note cards effectively	____/____	
■ Showed enthusiasm	____/____	
■ Evidence of preparation and practice	____/____	
Overall		
■ Maintained time parameters _____	____/____	
■ Effective selection, preparation and use of visual aid	____/____	
■ Personal involvement evident	____/____	

* SPEECH SCORE   ____/____

ASSIGNMENT #3

"What Do *You* Think?" Speech—Informative

Outline Grading Sheet

ATTACH THIS SHEET TO YOUR OUTLINE

Name _____ Section _____ Date _____

Criteria for grading your outline are as follows: Points/Score

Topic and Outline

- Chose subject appropriate to assignment   _____
- Wrote clear and narrow specific purpose   _____
- Used 3-column outline template   _____
- Wrote main and sub-points in complete sentences, word-processed   _____
- Proper coordination, subordination, symbolization, indentation   _____

Introduction—labeled

- Crafted and labeled all 5 parts of introduction   _____

Body—labeled

- Created 3 main points according to requirements—labeled   _____
- Developed each point fully, balanced   _____
- Wrote out transitions in complete sentences—labeled   _____
- Stated one idea per symbol   _____

Conclusion—labeled

- Crafted 2-part conclusion-labeled parts   _____

Over-all

- Note delivery or visual cues in 3rd column   _____
- Cited sources(s) on Works Cited page (MLA)   _____
- Note cards (Speaking Outline) reflects preparation outline   _____

TOTAL OUTLINE SCORE   _____

"WHAT DO *YOU* THINK?" SPEECH: PEER LISTENING SHEET (1)

Speaker _____   Listener _____

Section# _____   Topic _____

A. Audience adaptation

1. How did this speaker adapt this speech to you?

2. How could this speaker better adapt this speech to you and the rest of the audience?

B. Delivery

1. What were the two strongest aspects of delivery used by this speaker (example: eye contact, volume, rate, articulation, enthusiasm/sincerity, body language etc?).

2. Name one aspect of delivery the speaker should work on before the next speech.

C. Clarity of language and message

1. What are two ways this speaker made the message memorable enough so that you could tell it to someone else? (example: specific language use, transitions, organization, the audio-visual aids, etc.)

2. How could this speaker make the message clearer to you?

"WHAT DO *YOU* THINK?" SPEECH: PEER LISTENING SHEET (2)

Speaker _____   Listener _____

Section# _____   Topic _____

A. Audience adaptation

1. How did this speaker adapt this speech to you?

2. How could this speaker better adapt this speech to you and the rest of the audience?

B. Delivery

1. What were the two strongest aspects of delivery used by this speaker (example: eye contact, volume, rate, articulation, enthusiasm/sincerity, body language etc?).

2. Name one aspect of delivery the speaker should work on before the next speech.

C. Clarity of language and message

1. What are two ways this speaker made the message memorable enough so that you could tell it to someone else? (example: specific language use, transitions, organization, the audio-visual aids, etc.)

2. How could this speaker make the message clearer to you?

"What Do *You* Think?" Speech: Peer Listening sheet (3)

Speaker _____   Listener _____

Section# _____   Topic _____

A. Audience adaptation

1. How did this speaker adapt this speech to you?

2. How could this speaker better adapt this speech to you and the rest of the audience?

B. Delivery

1. What were the two strongest aspects of delivery used by this speaker (example: eye contact, volume, rate, articulation, enthusiasm/sincerity, body language etc?).

2. Name one aspect of delivery the speaker should work on before the next speech.

C.   Clarity of language and message

1. What are two ways this speaker made the message memorable enough so that you could tell it to someone else? (example: specific language use, transitions, organization, the audio-visual aids, etc.)

2. How could this speaker make the message clearer to you?

"WHAT DO *YOU* THINK?" SPEECH: PEER LISTENING SHEET (4)

Speaker _____   Listener _____

Section# _____   Topic _____

A. Audience adaptation

1. How did this speaker adapt this speech to you?

2. How could this speaker better adapt this speech to you and the rest of the audience?

B. Delivery

1. What were the two strongest aspects of delivery used by this speaker (example: eye contact, volume, rate, articulation, enthusiasm/sincerity, body language etc?).

2. Name one aspect of delivery the speaker should work on before the next speech.

C. Clarity of language and message

1. What are two ways this speaker made the message memorable enough so that you could tell it to someone else? (example: specific language use, transitions, organization, the audio-visual aids, etc.)

2. How could this speaker make the message clearer to you?

"What Do *You* Think?" Speech: Peer Listening sheet (5)

Speaker _____   Listener _____

Section# _____   Topic _____

A. Audience adaptation

1. How did this speaker adapt this speech to you?

2. How could this speaker better adapt this speech to you and the rest of the audience?

B. Delivery

1. What were the two strongest aspects of delivery used by this speaker (example: eye contact, volume, rate, articulation, enthusiasm/sincerity, body language etc?).

2. Name one aspect of delivery the speaker should work on before the next speech.

C.   Clarity of language and message

1. What are two ways this speaker made the message memorable enough so that you could tell it to someone else? (example: specific language use, transitions, organization, the audio-visual aids, etc.)

2. How could this speaker make the message clearer to you?

"What Do *You* Think?" Speech:
Peer Listening sheet (6)

Speaker _____   Listener _____

Section# _____   Topic _____

A. Audience adaptation

1. How did this speaker adapt this speech to you?

2. How could this speaker better adapt this speech to you and the rest of the audience?

B. Delivery

1. What were the two strongest aspects of delivery used by this speaker (example: eye contact, volume, rate, articulation, enthusiasm/sincerity, body language etc?).

2. Name one aspect of delivery the speaker should work on before the next speech.

C. Clarity of language and message

1. What are two ways this speaker made the message memorable enough so that you could tell it to someone else? (example: specific language use, transitions, organization, the audio-visual aids, etc.)

2. How could this speaker make the message clearer to you?

"WHAT DO *YOU* THINK?" SPEECH: PEER LISTENING SHEET (7)

Speaker _____ Listener _____

Section# _____ Topic _____

A. Audience adaptation

1. How did this speaker adapt this speech to you?

2. How could this speaker better adapt this speech to you and the rest of the audience?

B. Delivery

1. What were the two strongest aspects of delivery used by this speaker (example: eye contact, volume, rate, articulation, enthusiasm/sincerity, body language etc?).

2. Name one aspect of delivery the speaker should work on before the next speech.

C. Clarity of language and message

1. What are two ways this speaker made the message memorable enough so that you could tell it to someone else? (example: specific language use, transitions, organization, the audio-visual aids, etc.)

2. How could this speaker make the message clearer to you?

"WHAT DO *YOU* THINK?" SPEECH: SELF-EVALUATION SHEET

Directions

Review your speech from your videotape. Write an **essay** evaluating your performance based on the questions below. Be sure your work is typed or word-processed. See sample self-evaluation in this section of the book. Submit per instructor's directions.

- Did I spend enough time gathering information/preparing/practicing? Explain.

- Did I choose interesting information and was I creative with it? Give examples.

- Did I use my audio/visual aids effectively? Why or why not?

- Was my information appropriately organized? Explain.

- Did I make eye contact with the audience?

- Did I use appropriate body language? Give examples?

- Was I understandable? Was I enthusiastic?

- Did I achieve the time limits? Why or why not?

- How did I use my note cards? Be specific.

- I did the following things well and they were effective because: Cite evidence from Peer Evaluations as well as teacher response from Speaker Evaluation.

- The following things I did were ineffective because: Cite evidence from Peer Evaluations as well as teacher response from Speaker Evaluation.

- Here's what I intend to correct for the next speech and here's how I intend to do it:

"What Do You Think?" Speech

MEGAN GRANTZ

Megan Grantz
Section 2651
"What Do *You* Think?" Speech
Audience Analysis /Adaptation

Directions

Study the Listening Sheet you completed from the Introduction Speech. Based on the information you gathered by listening to the Introduction Speeches of your classmates and informal observations you may have made, answer the following questions: (TYPE OR WORD-PROCESS YOUR ANSWERS AND ESSAY ON A SEPARATE SHEET.)

1.   **What is the average age of your audience? What is the age range?** The ages range from nineteen to thirty-seven with the average age being about twenty-five.

2.   **How many males in your class? Females?** Most of the students in class were female. There is about a 73%/27% ratio of women to men in the class

3.   **Are there any non-native speakers? If so, how many and from where?** None

4.   **How many of your classmates are married? How many have children?** Several students were single or dating while others are married with families.

5.   **Can you name 2 or 3 things that the majority of your classmates have in common?** Most everyone wants to graduate from college to better their lives and accomplish a goal. For the majority of us the path to receiving a higher education has been long and many students have other obligations such as work and family. Therefore, classes are taken on a part-time basis.

6.   **If a friend asked you to describe your classmates in R110, how would you describe them as a group?** Rather traditional. While our class does not represent physical or cultural diversity, per se, there are certain careers and lifestyles that are unique and will cause us to reflect more profoundly on our choices of topic.

7.   **In essay form tell why you think that this topic may be important to your audience (cite any relevant attitudes, beliefs, demographic or situational characteristics to back up your thoughts.) Also, as you look over your answers to the questions above, how can you use this information to craft a speech that is relevant/beneficial/interesting to your classmates?**
We have a traditional and rather conservative and non-diverse class. Since this movie (Napoleon Dynamite) was such an odd and polarizing film, I thought it would be beneficial to look up some of the history and circumstances around its development and release so that it would have a little more credibility with the audience. Also, I thought that some humor would help. The quote I will use from the Idaho state legislature bill that was passed regarding the movie, was really cute and I am hoping that it will be a good attention-getter that puts the movie into a larger perspective for the class.

Student's Name: Megan Grantz
R110—Section No. 2651

"What Do *You* Think?" Speech #3
Movie: "Napoleon Dynamite"

Specific Purpose: To inform my R110 audience how the idea of friendship from the movie, "Napoleon Dynamite" has impacted me.

Central Idea: The friendship between Napoleon and Pedro is highlighted in three scenes of the movie and has given me a different perspective on the idea of friendship, and can cause you to become more appreciative of your own friendships.

LEFT COLUMN Label speech function	MIDDLE COLUMN Content of speech *Written in Complete Sentences/Phrases*	RIGHT COLUMN Label physical behaviors
	INTRODUCTION	
Attention	I. The following is from an interview with the senator of Idaho and is included in a bill recently passed in Idaho, "Whereas, any members of the House of Representatives or the Legislature of the State of Idaho who chooses to vote 'Nay' on this concurrent resolution are 'freakin' idiots!' and run the risk of having the 'Worst Day of Their Lives!' This bill is a resolution to commend the movie "Napoleon Dynamite." (Idaho Dynamite)	
Source		
Reveal Topic	II. As you can see this movie has had an impact on many people in this nation as well as myself. In fact I have a completely different view on friendship now because of the movie.	
Relevancy	III. Friendship is a very important aspect of all of our lives. The idea of friendship can sometimes be a hard concept for many to grasp. Watching "Napoleon Dynamite" can help you to understand friendships a little better.	
Credibility	IV. After watching this movie I feel that I appreciate my friends, who you see in this picture, a lot more than before.	
Preview	V. The friendship between Napoleon and Pedro is highlighted in three scenes of the movie; these scenes have given me a different perspective on the idea of friendship, and can cause you to become more appreciative of your own friendships.	Show picture

	BODY	
Main Point	I. Napoleon and Pedro have a unique relationship which is portrayed in three scenes of Napoleon Dynamite.	Eye contact with audience!
Sub-Point Sub-Sub-Point	A. The first scene takes place at the school dance.	
	1. Napoleon found himself taking a popular girl to the dance after she was forced into it by her mother.	
	2. The girl left Napoleon at the dance alone so that she could be with her friends.	
	3. Aware of what has happened, Pedro lets Napoleon have a dance with his date Deb.	
	B. The second scene began with Pedro becoming very hot after realizing that his competition for school president was Summer, the most popular girl in school.	
	1. After trying different tactics to cool down Pedro decides that the problem is his hair so he shaves it off.	
	2. After Pedro tells Napoleon that he is insecure about being bald, Napoleon finds a wig for Pedro to wear.	
	C. The last scene is the famous dance by Napoleon.	
	1. The candidate speeches were taking place and Pedro had been informed that he needed a skit.	
	2. Pedro got discouraged by this fact because it was too late to come up with one.	
	3. Knowing this, Napoleon decides to go on stage and dance in front of the whole school by himself.	
TRANSITION	Now I will talk about how theses scenes impacted me.	
Main Point	II. After watching these scenes I realized that my definition of friendship does not hold true for everyone.	
Sub-Point	A. I used to believe that friends never run out of things to talk about, have many common interests, will always stick up for one another, and can laugh together at just about anything.	
	B. What I didn't realize is that this is only true for me and my friends. The friendship between Napoleon and Pedro only has one of those aspects and that is sticking up for each other.	
Sub-Sub-Point	1. Although you do see a few common interests between Napoleon and Pedro they are few and far between.	

Source	2. Despite this lack of friendship-like qualities, their friendship remains strong. 3. There appears to be an unspoken understanding between the two that digs deeper than any superficial definition of friendship currently known. C. I now understand what Robert Scotellaro, an author of children's books, meant when he said, "There are no blueprints for friendship, each one is custom made." (Craig web) D. A friendship can only be defined by the people in it and that definition is not the same for every other friendship.	
TRANSITION	Now that you know how Napoleon and Pedro's friendship has impacted me, I will talk about how you can be affected as well.	
Main Point Sub-Point Sub-Sub-Point	III. After taking a closer look at the bond between Napoleon and Pedro you might find yourself becoming more appreciative of your own friendships. A. Napoleon and Pedro are willing to stand by each other through thick and thin. 1. This is true for almost all friendships. 2. You can probably think of a time when your own friends came running to your rescue, maybe a loved one had just died, or you had broken up with your boyfriend or girlfriend, or maybe you were just embarrassed. B. Friendship is a strong bond that many people tend to take for granted but if you realize all the time that your friendships have brought you out of a rut, you'll begin to think differently.	
Review Exit Line	**CONCLUSION** I. "Napoleon Dynamite" may seem like a movie to watch for pure entertainment but it has many underlying themes that people can learn from. From three scenes I learned that there is more to friendship than I had previously thought and this has changed my attitude towards friendship. You, too, can learn more about your own friendships from this movie. II. Hopefully when you leave here today you will all realize how important each individual friendship is to you and will cherish them as they deserve to be.	

Works Cited

Craig's Quotations about Life. December 20, 1997. October 5, 2005
  <http://www.csbruce.com/~csbruce/quotes/life.html>

Idaho Dynamite. (n.d.) Studio 360. October 5, 2005
  <http://www.wnyc.org/studio360/commentary.html>

Megan Grantz
"What Do *You* Think?" Speech—Self-Evaluation

After reflecting on my speech and the comments I received I feel as though I did a better job than what I originally thought I would. I was very stressed about this speech, mainly because I struggled with my outline. After watching my tape I was pleasantly surprised at how well I did. One thing that I feel I did extremely well was maintain eye contact with my audience. It seemed as though I was speaking directly to them with a purpose, not just speaking to get a good grade. I realized that I enunciated (this tends to be a huge problem for me) and my volume was good.

Although I was generally very happy with my speech I realized there are areas I need to work on. My biggest problem I believe at this point is citing my sources. I'm usually very good at this and somehow this became my biggest problem. Also, while I was speaking I thought I kept a very good pace, but after watching my tape I found that I started to speed up towards the end. Another issue of mine was actually writing the outline. I got a comment that my speech wasn't organized and I immediately disagreed, but after thinking about I've decided that just because my speech seemed organized to me that doesn't mean it will be to everyone else.

Before the next speech I need to work on writing an effective outline. This means starting early and going to the speaker's lab for help if needed. Also I need to work on my delivery, which also includes going to the speaker's lab. I need to video tape myself giving the speech and address my problem areas before my final presentation. Next I need to figure out what to put on my key word outline so that I don't draw a blank again.

Like I said, overall I was very pleased with my speech but I know that there is always room for improvement.

THE DEMONSTRATION SPEECH

What Is a Demonstration Speech and Why Is it Required?

Your experience with preparing this type of speech will help you in showing others how something is done, is made, works, or is fixed in an organized, easily remembered way. Your purpose is to describe so thoroughly what you are doing and to physically demonstrate a process using actual materials (or visuals or representative models), that your audience members can replicate your demonstration. The emphasis in this speech is on demonstrating how to **perform a process. The time allowed for this speech is 5–7 minutes.**

The audience expectation and response after hearing your Demonstration Speech should include the following:

- This is interesting.

- This is a beneficial process/skill; I should know how to do this.

- I *want* to know how to do this.

- If I had all the materials in front of me, I have learned enough from this speech that I could do/perform this task.

What Skills You Will Learn

1. You will learn how to **select a topic** that is beneficial to your audience.

2. You will learn to **construct a specific purpose** to guide your speech.

3. You will **perform basic research** for your topic. *(Minimum of three sources)*

4. You will learn to **organize your material** in an easy-to-understand manner.

5. You will **practice using audio-visual aids.**

6. You will practice using **descriptive language.**

7. You will practice **adapting your material** to your audience.

8. You will practice appropriate aspects of **delivery.**

Sample Topics

- **How to tie three simple knots**
- **How to properly wrap a package for mailing**
- **How to glue a wood joint**
- How to jump-start a car with booster cables
- How to sew on a button so it won't come off
- How to take a blood pressure
- How to repair drywall
- How to clean your CD player, VCR, computer
- How to filet a fish, cut up a chicken

What Are the Requirements for This Speech?

1. **A beneficial topic** for your audience

2. A **clear specific purpose and central idea**

3. Completed **Audience Analysis/Adaptation Sheet**

4. A typed or word-processed **preparation outline** with the following functions labeled:
   - **introduction and parts**
   - **body and parts**
   - **conclusion and parts**
   - **transitions written out**
   - **physical behaviors listed (use of audio-visual aids) in right hand column**
   - **Works Cited and Works Consulted** (as required by your instructor)

5. **At least 2 audio-visual aids**

6. At least **3 sources (books, periodicals, interviews, etc.—one of these must be a NON-INTERNET source),** orally cited and noted on your Works Cited page (MLA format)

7. **2 note cards** to be *turned in* after your speech

8. Time requirement of **5–7 minutes**

9. **Self-evaluation** turned in according to instructor's deadline.

10. Other _____

Task Checklist: (✔ Check Off as You Complete Each One)

❏ 1. Using your **Audience Analysis/Adaptation Sheet,** choose a subject beneficial to **this** audience and with which you have had *experience.*

❏ 2. Construct your **specific purpose** with your audience in mind.

❏ 3. Research your purpose.

❏ 4. **Create your preparation outline.**

❏ 5. **Choose/create your visuals.** Ask:

   ▪ What does the audience need to see, feel, touch, hear, smell, in order to understand how to perform this process?

   ▪ How much do I have to show and describe (consider a modified demo)?

   ▪ Save your visuals to RESOURCES in Oncourse CL. Bring visuals to class on a flash drive or CDROM.

❏ 6. **Practice** from your preparation outline. Time yourself.

❏ 7. **Practice** with your audio-visual aids. Time yourself.

❏ 8. **Create your note cards.** *DO NOT write out your speech or preparation outline word-for-word on your note cards!* **Practice** with audio-visuals. **Time** yourself. **Edit** if necessary.

❏ 9. **Assess room situation** for speech and come prepared.

❏ 10. Be able to **set up quickly** and deliver speech. Be able to **tear down quickly.**

❏ 11. Give your instructor your **preparation outline with Outline Grading Sheet attached, the audience analysis, and both Speaker Evaluation Sheets** before you speak.

❏ 12. After your speech, **view** your videotape. Thoughtfully write your **Self-Evaluation Essay** and submit to your instructor by deadline.

Grading Criteria

Grading Criteria for this Speech: See the Speaker Evaluation form and the Outline Grading Sheet in the Coursebook. *Apply these criteria to what you have prepared in order to optimize your grade points.*

Demonstration Speech: Audience Analysis/Adaptation

Directions

Study the Listening Sheet and the Audience Analysis of your class that you completed from the Introduction Speech in your Coursebook. Based on the information you gathered by listening to the Introduction Speeches of your classmates and on any surveys or informal observations you may have made of your classmates so far, answer the following questions: (TYPE OR WORD-PROCESS YOUR ANSWERS AND ESSAY ON A SEPARATE SHEET. Submit per your instructor's directions).

My Speech to Demonstrate Specific Purpose is_____.

Demographic Audience Information

1. What is the average age of the audience? What is the age range?

2. How many males are in the class? Females?

3. Are there any non-native speakers? If so, how many and from where?

4. How many of your classmates are married? How many are divorced? How many have kids?

5. List some of the interests and hobbies held by audience.

6. Can you name 2 or 3 things that the majority of your classmates have in common?

7. If a friend asked you to describe your classmates in R110, how would you describe them as a group?

Speech Adaptation

8. In essay form, tell why your audience will want to know about or be able to perform the demonstration you are considering. Cite relevant demographic characteristics from the information above.

9. Discuss any adaptations you will need to make to the speech content or physical circumstances so that your demonstration will be clearer to the audience.

ASSIGNMENT #4

Demonstration Speech—Informative

Speaker Evaluation Sheet

I visited the Speaker's Lab for this assignment. Circle one.   **YES   NO**

Name _____ Section _____ Date _____

Specific Purpose and Central Idea (SP/CI) _____

_____

	Points/Score	Comments

Introduction
- Gained attention/interest ____/____
- Revealed topic clearly (SP) ____/____
- Showed relevance to audience ____/____
- Established speaker credibility ____/____
- Previewed body of speech (CI) ____/____

Body
- Main points presented clearly ____/____
- Main points presented in effective organizational pattern ____/____
- Main points limited and easy to follow ____/____
- Visual aids selected, prepared and used effectively ____/____
- Researched material strongly supports main points ____/____

Conclusion
- Audience prepared for conclusion ____/____
- Process summarized/reviewed ____/____
- Closed with circular constructions or other device ____/____

Delivery
- Used extemporaneous delivery style ____/____
- Maintained eye contact with audience throughout demo ____/____
- Used body and space effectively during demo ____/____
- Used voice effectively ____/____
  (vol., rate, pitch, artic., voc. pauses, etc.)
- Used note cards effectively ____/____
- Evidence of preparation and practice ____/____
- Personal enthusiasm evident ____/____

Overall
- Maintained time parameters _____ ____/____
- Demo so thorough that audience could repeat ____/____
- Adapted material and technique to audience/situation ____/____
- Sources effectively cited and sufficient number (3) ____/____

* SPEECH SCORE ____/____

ASSIGNMENT #4

Demonstration Speech—Informative

Speaker Evaluation Sheet

I visited the Speaker's Lab for this assignment. Circle one.   **YES**   **NO**

Name _____   Section _____   Date _____

Specific Purpose and Central Idea (SP/CI) _____

_____

	Points/Score	Comments

Introduction
▪ Gained attention/interest   ____/____
▪ Revealed topic clearly (SP)   ____/____
▪ Showed relevance to audience   ____/____
▪ Established speaker credibility   ____/____
▪ Previewed body of speech (CI)   ____/____

Body
▪ Main points presented clearly   ____/____
▪ Main points presented in effective organizational pattern   ____/____
▪ Main points limited and easy to follow   ____/____
▪ Visual aids selected, prepared and used effectively   ____/____
▪ Researched material strongly supports main points   ____/____

Conclusion
▪ Audience prepared for conclusion   ____/____
▪ Process summarized/reviewed   ____/____
▪ Closed with circular constructions or other device   ____/____

Delivery
▪ Used extemporaneous delivery style   ____/____
▪ Maintained eye contact with audience throughout demo   ____/____
▪ Used body and space effectively during demo   ____/____
▪ Used voice effectively   ____/____
  (vol., rate, pitch, artic., voc. pauses, etc.)
▪ Used note cards effectively   ____/____
▪ Evidence of preparation and practice   ____/____
▪ Personal enthusiasm evident   ____/____

Overall
▪ Maintained time parameters _____   ____/____
▪ Demo so thorough that audience could repeat   ____/____
▪ Adapted material and technique to audience/situation   ____/____
▪ Sources effectively cited and sufficient number (3)   ____/____

* SPEECH SCORE   ____/____

ASSIGNMENT #4

Demonstration Speech—Informative

Outline Grading Sheet

ATTACH THIS SHEET TO YOUR OUTLINE

Name _____ **Section** _____ **Date** _____

Criteria for grading your outline are as follows:　　　　　　　　Points/Score

Topic/Format
- Chose subject appropriate to assignment　　　　　　　　　_____
- Wrote narrow, clear SP and CI　　　　　　　　　_____
- Used 3-column template—word processed　　　　　　　　　_____
- Proper coordination, subordination, symbolization, indentation　_____
- Wrote clear main and sub-points in complete sentences　_____
- Sources cited on Works Cited page (MLA)　　　　　　　　　_____

Introduction—labeled
- Effectively crafted and labeled all 5 parts of introduction　_____

Body—labeled
- Used appropriate organizational pattern of main
  points—pattern labeled　　　　　　　　　_____
- Developed main points fully, vividly　　　　　　　　　_____
- Physical cues for demonstration indicated in 3rd column　_____
- Transitions written out in complete sentences—labeled　_____
- Stated one idea per symbol.　　　　　　　　　_____

Conclusion—labeled
- Crafted 2-part ending—labeled　　　　　　　　　_____

Over-all
- Note cards (Key Word Outline) reflects preparation outline　_____

TOTAL OUTLINE SCORE　　　　　　　　　_____

Demonstration Speech: Peer Listening Sheet (1)

Speaker _____ Listener _____

Section# _____ Topic _____

A. Audience adaptation

1. List **one** way that this speaker attempted to adapt the content of the speech to this audience.

2. Provide at least one constructive suggestion for how the audience adaptation in this speech could be improved.

B. Delivery

1. In the space provided below, evaluate this speaker's delivery, including such aspects as eye contact, volume, rate, articulation, enthusiasm, gestures, and posture.

2. What single aspect of delivery should the speaker work on before the next speech?

3. Discuss a way in which the speaker made the demonstration clear enough for you to be able to repeat the steps (use of visuals, explanation of steps, etc.).

4. Give suggestions as to how the speaker could have made the demonstration more clear to you.

Demonstration Speech: Peer Listening Sheet (2)

Speaker _____ Listener _____

Section# _____ Topic _____

A. Audience adaptation

1. List **one** way that this speaker attempted to adapt the content of the speech to this audience.

2. Provide at least one constructive suggestion for how the audience adaptation in this speech could be improved.

B. Delivery

1. In the space provided below, evaluate this speaker's delivery, including such aspects as eye contact, volume, rate, articulation, enthusiasm, gestures, and posture.

2. What single aspect of delivery should the speaker work on before the next speech?

3. Discuss a way in which the speaker made the demonstration clear enough for you to be able to repeat the steps (use of visuals, explanation of steps, etc.).

4. Give suggestions as to how the speaker could have made the demonstration more clear to you.

DEMONSTRATION SPEECH: PEER LISTENING SHEET (3)

Speaker _____ Listener _____

Section# _____ Topic _____

A. Audience adaptation

1. List **one** way that this speaker attempted to adapt the content of the speech to this audience.

2. Provide at least one constructive suggestion for how the audience adaptation in this speech could be improved.

B. Delivery

1. In the space provided below, evaluate this speaker's delivery, including such aspects as eye contact, volume, rate, articulation, enthusiasm, gestures, and posture.

2. What single aspect of delivery should the speaker work on before the next speech?

3. Discuss a way in which the speaker made the demonstration clear enough for you to be able to repeat the steps (use of visuals, explanation of steps, etc.).

4. Give suggestions as to how the speaker could have made the demonstration more clear to you.

DEMONSTRATION SPEECH: PEER LISTENING SHEET (4)

Speaker _____   Listener _____

Section# _____   Topic _____

A. Audience adaptation

1. List **one** way that this speaker attempted to adapt the content of the speech to this audience.

2. Provide at least one constructive suggestion for how the audience adaptation in this speech could be improved.

B. Delivery

1. In the space provided below, evaluate this speaker's delivery, including such aspects as eye contact, volume, rate, articulation, enthusiasm, gestures, and posture.

2. What single aspect of delivery should the speaker work on before the next speech?

3. Discuss a way in which the speaker made the demonstration clear enough for you to be able to repeat the steps (use of visuals, explanation of steps, etc.).

4. Give suggestions as to how the speaker could have made the demonstration more clear to you.

DEMONSTRATION SPEECH:
PEER LISTENING SHEET (5)

Speaker _____ Listener _____

Section# _____ Topic _____

A. Audience adaptation

1. List **one** way that this speaker attempted to adapt the content of the speech to this audience.

2. Provide at least one constructive suggestion for how the audience adaptation in this speech could be improved.

B. Delivery

1. In the space provided below, evaluate this speaker's delivery, including such aspects as eye contact, volume, rate, articulation, enthusiasm, gestures, and posture.

2. What single aspect of delivery should the speaker work on before the next speech?

3. Discuss a way in which the speaker made the demonstration clear enough for you to be able to repeat the steps (use of visuals, explanation of steps, etc.).

4. Give suggestions as to how the speaker could have made the demonstration more clear to you.

Demonstration Speech:
Peer Listening Sheet (6)

Speaker _____ Listener _____

Section# _____ Topic _____

A. Audience adaptation

1. List **one** way that this speaker attempted to adapt the content of the speech to this audience.

2. Provide at least one constructive suggestion for how the audience adaptation in this speech could be improved.

B. Delivery

1. In the space provided below, evaluate this speaker's delivery, including such aspects as eye contact, volume, rate, articulation, enthusiasm, gestures, and posture.

2. What single aspect of delivery should the speaker work on before the next speech?

3. Discuss a way in which the speaker made the demonstration clear enough for you to be able to repeat the steps (use of visuals, explanation of steps, etc.).

4. Give suggestions as to how the speaker could have made the demonstration more clear to you.

DEMONSTRATION SPEECH: PEER LISTENING SHEET (7)

Speaker _____   Listener _____

Section# _____   Topic _____

A. Audience adaptation

1. List **one** way that this speaker attempted to adapt the content of the speech to this audience.

2. Provide at least one constructive suggestion for how the audience adaptation in this speech could be improved.

B. Delivery

1. In the space provided below, evaluate this speaker's delivery, including such aspects as eye contact, volume, rate, articulation, enthusiasm, gestures, and posture.

2. What single aspect of delivery should the speaker work on before the next speech?

3. Discuss a way in which the speaker made the demonstration clear enough for you to be able to repeat the steps (use of visuals, explanation of steps, etc.).

4. Give suggestions as to how the speaker could have made the demonstration more clear to you

DEMONSTRATION SPEECH: SELF-EVALUATION SHEET

Directions

Review your speech from your video tape. Write a **reflective narrative** evaluating your perform-ance and basing your comments on your thoughtful responses to the concerns and issues below. Be sure your work is typed or word-processed. Submit per instructor's directions. See sample demonstration self-evaluation in the section following.

- Did I spend enough time gathering information/preparing/practicing? Explain.

- Did I choose interesting information and was I creative with it? Give examples.

- Did I use audio/visual aids effectively? Why or why not?

- Is it likely the audience could do the demonstration themselves after seeing my speech? Explain.

- Was my information appropriately organized? Explain.

- Did I make eye contact with the audience?

- Did I use appropriate body language? Give examples?

- Was I understandable? Was I enthusiastic?

- Did I achieve the time limits? Why or why not?

- How did I use my note cards? Be specific.

- I did the following things well and they were effective because: Cite evidence from Peer Evaluations as well as teacher response from Speaker Evaluation.

- The following things I did were ineffective because: Cite evidence from Peer Evaluations as well as teacher response from Speaker Evaluation.

- Here's what I intend to correct for the next speech and here's how I intend to do it:

- Despite everything, here are some things which I am consistently doing better, most of the time.

THE DEMONSTRATION SPEECH

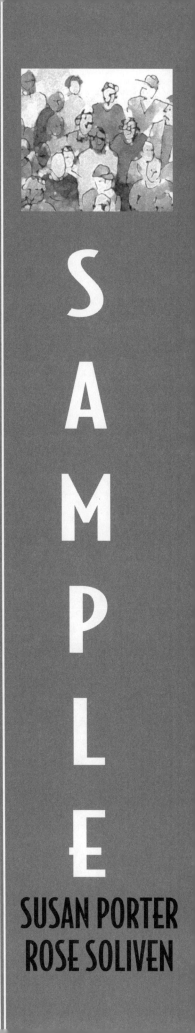

SAMPLE

SUSAN PORTER
ROSE SOLIVEN

These documents are examples of student work. They are included to give you an idea of how to prepare your speech materials and the quality of work expected. All student work is printed with student permission and is subject to U.S. copyright law.

Susan Porter
R110/Section 448
Speaker #25

Audience Analysis

Possible Speech Topic: Stenciling

Approximately 70% of the students in my public speaking class, section 448, are 16-20 years of age. The ages of the students range from 19 years of age to 39 years of age. There are seven males in class and seventeen females.

There are two students who may be non-native speakers. One student appears to be of Hispanic origin. The other student is from the Philippines.

An overwhelming majority of the students in class are single. Two students are engaged. Three of the students are married and have children. One student is divorced.

Some interests and hobbies of my classmates are traveling, sports, hiking and camping, painting, drawing, dance, gardening, and reading. A majority of my classmates like to participate in sports. Some of the sports mentioned in their introduction speeches include tennis, weight lifting, running, hiking, and riding horses. Another similarity of the majority of my classmates is disliking rude, inconsiderate people. The most important thing that the majority of my classmates have in common is their age.

There aren't any beliefs or attitudes of my classmates that significantly relate to my topic. I remember, however, starting out with a new job, living in a new place, and wanting my new place to feel like home. The majority of my classmates will soon be at that point in their lives. Several students mentioned in their introduction speeches that they like making money. I'm assuming that they like making money, so they can buy and do things with that money. My classmates will like to hear about a cost-effective way to make their new places seem like home, so their money can be spent on more important items. Stenciling, as an option for decorating, is an easy way to personalize their place and it is not expensive.

First, I'll show my classmates how easy it would be to add character to their place by stenciling. I'll emphasize that you can be as creative as you want with stenciling, which hopefully will keep the interest of the students who are artistic. Next, I'll compare the costs of wallpaper versus stenciling, which will illustrate that stenciling is an inexpensive decorating option. I imagine the cost savings will be what the males in the class remember

SAMPLE DEMONSTRATION SPEECH PREPARATION OUTLINE

Susan Porter
R110—Section No. B448

Specific Purpose: To demonstrate to my R110 audience that stenciling is an easy, cost-effective way to personalize your home.

Central Idea: By following 5 preparatory steps, stenciling can be done easily on a prepared surface in 5 additional steps.

LEFT COLUMN Label speech function	MIDDLE COLUMN Content of speech *UseComplete Sentences*	RIGHT COLUMN Label physical behaviors
	INTRODUCTION	
Attention	I. I can't draw, I can't paint pictures, and I can't sew. I am just not a creative person. I did, however, just finish painting this design along two walls of my bedroom.	(Show drywall with stenciled design)
Reveal Topic	II. This was done by stenciling which is according to Janet Waring who authored Early American Stencils on Wall and Furniture, "a cut out pattern through which design is applied to a surface in contrasting color." (Waring, 2)	
Relevancy	III. Most of you in a few years will be starting out with a new job and your own place now. Stenciling is a good decorating option to remember when you want to easily add some personalization to your place but you don't want to spend a lot of money.	
Credibility	IV. I have stenciled 10 rooms and a couple pieces of furniture over the years. The results have always been very pleasing. Basically, if I can stencil anyone should be able to.	
Preview	V. In my talk today, I will explain what you need to prepare to stencil, how to stencil, and the benefits of stenciling.	

	BODY	
Main Point	I. There are five basic preparatory steps needed for stenciling.	(Show basic and overlays)

Sub-Point
Sub-Sub-Point
	A. Choose the design and complexity of the stencil.
	     1. Basic
	     2. Overlays
	     3. Make-your-own	

	B. Choose the colors of paint.
	   C. Decide which tools you will use to apply paint.
	     1. Brushes
	     2. Sponges
		(Point out paints)
		(Show brush and sponge)

	D. Prepare the surface to be stenciled.
	   E. Collected extra needed items from around the house.
	     1. Palette
	     2. Paper Towels
	     3. Tape
	     4. Cotton Swabs
	     5. Background color
		(Indicate extra items)

Transition	Now, that you know what materials are needed, you are ready to learn how to stencil.	

Main Point
Sub-Point
	II. There are five basic steps in stenciling.
	   A. First, tape stencil to prepared surface.
	   B. Second, make palette of paints.
	   C. Third, dampen sponges; load on color; remove excess.
	   D. Fourth, color opening in the stencil and remove.
	   E. Fifth, clean up an unwanted color.
		(Demonstrate steps)

Transition	Now, you know the materials needed for stenciling and you know basically how to stencil. You have seen how easy it would be to personalize your home with stenciling. Now, let's look at the other major benefit of stenciling.	

Main Point
 	
Sub-Point
 	
Sub-Sub-Point
	III. Stenciling has always been a cost-effective way to decorate your home.
	   A. Stenciling directly on walls as an option for decorating started on the 1700's in colonial America.
	     1. Wallpaper cost
	     2. "For a small fee and board and lodging"
	   B. Stenciling on walls is still popular today,
	     1. Wallpaper cost
	     2. Stenciling cost
		(Show transparency)

Sub-Point	C. As companies have increased the choices in colors and designs, stenciling has become even more popular. Some companies now sell stencil kits, which included your stencils and paint together. Plaid Enterprises' president, Michael McCooey, remarked, "The manufacturer does 90% of the work, the consumer 10% but they can take all the credit." (Forbes, March 1996)
Restate purpose (review of Main Points)

Clincher/tag/exit line or Final Appeal | **CONCLUSION**
I. You have seen how easy it is to stencil. All you need is a design, paints, sponges, and something to be decorated. You have seen how stenciling, since colonial America, can be cost-effective way to personalize a room.
II. So, when you are ready to "bring color into the how", as Janet Waring, author of Early American Stencils on wall and Furniture, states, think of stenciling "it requires no outstanding skill." (Waring, 20-23) Look at me! |

Works Cited

Rossand, Julilette. ""Somewhat individual": want to do something creative, but in a hurry? Some clever marketers have just the products for you." Forbes 157 (March 1996): 156

Slayton, Marietta Paine. Early American Decorating Techniques. New York, NY: the Macmillan Company, 1972.

Waring, Janet, Early American Stencils on Walls and Furniture. New York, NY: Dover Publications, Inc., 1968.

Susan Porter
R110/Section 448
Demonstration Speech—Self-Evaluation

I spent enough time gathering information and preparing for my speech. Finding appropriate quotes took some time. The hardest part in preparing for the speech was trying to decide what information to share and what to leave out. I spent quite a bit of time practicing my speech. I had too much information and needed it to flow smoothly in the allotted time, so I practiced and practiced. I never once said my speech in less than seven minutes when I practiced.

I wanted to include some of the history of stenciling because I thought it was interesting. I made a transparency of a stenciled colonial wall to give my classmates an idea of 1) what stenciling was like then and 2) to give them an idea of how creative they could be with stenciling now.

I thought the overhead was effective, as I showed it at a time in my speech when I was saying a lot of words and had nothing visual. My demonstration of stenciling was effective. I verbally listed the steps a couple of times as I demonstrated, plus gave some experience tips. I do think the audience could stencil themselves. The steps were listed in a chronological manner—one step follows another.

My information was appropriately organized. I explained what stenciling is, and then went on to materials needed, then how to stencil, and last why you should stencil.

I thought my eye contact and body language were good. I tried to focus longer on each person with my eye contact. I thought that I looked pretty natural with my gestures and moved to both sides of the room well.

I'm an enthusiastic person, so that part comes naturally. I did speak rather fast at the beginning. My first quote was rather cumbersome and hard to understand, so I flew through it, so that I could explain it in my own words. I was also concerned about making the time limit. I did finish in 6:25, but that was mostly because I forgot several items.

I used my note cards only to make sure that my quotes were accurate. When I practiced at home, I mainly worked on my introduction, transitions, and conclusion. I figured if I knew those by heart, I could wing the rest.

My organization and presentation were effective because it was easy to follow and delivered with enthusiasm. I could tell from the videotape that my breathing is still a problem. I did not have a sore throat. When I'm up in front though, it feels like my tongue is twice the size and it is a labor to articulate well. I don't think of my breathing when I'm talking, I'm just thankful that I still am breathing!

I suppose that I'll try to control my gulping for air, though I'm not sure how. I will try to have more natural pauses in my next speech, so that means I can't have as much information. Hopefully during the pause, I can take a nice deep breath, not say "um" and continue on.

Student: R. Soliven
Demonstration Speech
COMM R110 Fundamentals of Speech Communication

Audience Analysis

Possible speech topic: Filipino bamboo stick dance

According to the information presented in my classmates' introduction speeches, at least 10 of the 26 students are 16 to 20 years old. However, the age range for the whole class spans from the 16-20 age bracket to the over 30 years-of-age bracket. The class consists of 11 male students and 16 female students.

There appears to be one student who is a non-native speaker, and he is originally from Mexico.

According the information presented in the speeches, two students are married, one student is divorced, and one student has children. However, several students did mention that they were engaged or had significant others.

From what I gathered from the introduction speeches, I have concluded that my classmates are fascinating people who have a variety of interests and hobbies. Many of my classmates enjoy music and play instruments, like the piano, flute, recorder, guitar, and harmonica. Other interests and hobbies include dancing, reading, traveling, running, and movies.

Similarities that a majority of my classmates share include a love of sports and enjoying life. Having an active lifestyle is important to many of my classmates, and some sports mentioned by some of my classmates were bowling, skating, drag racing, basketball, football, baseball, soccer, dancing, and running. My classmates also expressed an interest in enjoying life and having fun. Students mentioned that they liked learning, working hard, challenges and puzzles, traveling, and spending time with friends and family.

If I were to describe the students in my speech class to a friend, I would say that they are a highly interesting, diverse, and motivated group of people who have various life experiences, interests, and life goals. However, despite their differences, they seem to possess perseverance and value hard work.

I think that my topic-demonstrating how to perform a Filipino bamboo stick dance-would be interesting and meaningful to my audience because the dance is an activity that may teach them about a different country's culture. Several students in my class expressed that they enjoyed traveling and experiencing new things, and seeing a demonstration speech about a dance from the Philippines could be an enriching learning experience. Students may discover something new about the Filipino culture and may be inspired to learn something about their own heritage or about another culture. Also, many students mentioned that they liked to stay active, and the dance I will demonstrate requires an interest in dance and lots of energy. Using the information gathered from the audience analysis, I can include information about how the dance is interesting to both Filipinos and non-Filipinos alike and how this dance reflects aspects of a foreign country's way of life.

Student's Name: R. Soliven
Title of Speech - Bamboo dance
Specific Purpose: To demonstrate for my class how to dance the *tinikling,* a Filipino folk dance.
Central Idea: The *tinikling,* a dance originating in the Philippines, is performed with 3 props and 4 basic steps.

	INTRODUCTION	
Attention	I. Imagine you are jumping in between rapidly moving bamboo poles on the ground. The poles click loudly together, and with each click, you fear the sticks will snap your feet off. Is this some strange torture mechanism? Or, could it be something else?	
Reveal Topic	II. This scenario describes a Filipino folk dance called the *tinikling,* and today, I will demonstrate how to dance the tinikling.	Show picture of *tinikling,* and then remove.
Relevancy	III. Since we live in a very diverse world, learning a dance from a different country can be an enriching, cultural experience for anyone. In addition, the tinikling is a fun, energetic activity for people of all ages.	
Credibility	IV. For 15 years, I have been performing Filipino dances for various events, like cultural festivals, weddings, and parties.	
Preview	V. In this speech, I will provide background information about the *tinikling,* describe the materials you will need for the dance, and finally teach you a few of the steps.	
	BODY	
Main Point	I. The *tinikling* has an interesting origin and continues to fascinate people today.	
Sub-Point	A. The dance comes from the central islands of the Philippines.	
	1. It is a quick-paced dance that requires balance and agility.	
	2. According to the book, *Sayaw-Philippine Dances,* by Reynaldo Alejandro, the dance movements imitate a bird called the *tinikling* bird as it "hops to escape bamboo traps amidst rice stalks." (Alejandro, 39)	
Sub-Point	B. The *tinikling* is considered the Philippines' national dance and is valued by Filipinos and non-Filipinos alike.	
	1. Eleanor Carino, a 19-year-old member of the Filipino American Community of South Puget Sound in Washington, states that	

	"dancing is a way for young people to involved in preserving Filipino culture." (Huber, 1) 2. And from a non-Filipino point of view, Marion Rex, a teacher at St. Marguerite School in Alberta, Canada, started a project at her school, which involved teaching high school students the tinikling in order to "develop an appreciation for a variety of dances." ("Spotlight," par. 2)	
Transition	So now that you understand a little about the origins of the dance, I will describe the props you will need to perform it.	

Main Point
 	
Sub-point
Sub-sub point
	II. Along with dancers and music, there are three 'props' used for performing the *tinikling*.
	  A. First, you will need two long poles.
	      1. Typically they are 8 feet long, but it depends on the number of dancers.
	      2. If you want to be authentic, bamboo poles are preferred.
	  B. Second, you need two small pieces of wood that you would put beneath the poles to help the dancers hear the clicking beat.
	  C. Third, you need duct tape, which is necessary to keep the small, wooden pieces from moving around during the dance.
		Pick up items as you describe them.

Transition	So now that know the props needed, I will teach you some dance steps. May I have my two volunteers to come up please?	Have Andy and Andrew come up.

Main Point
 	
Sub-Point
Sub-sub point
	III. These are four basic *tinikling* steps based on "in, in, out" with each dance step having three counts to it.
	  A. This is the first basic step.
	      1. Put your right foot in between the sticks as you lift your left foot off the ground.
	      2. Next land on your left foot as you lift your right foot.
	      3. Then you land on your right foot outside of the sticks and lift your left foot as the sticks click together.
	  B. The second basic step is the "cross-over" step— you keep the same foot in for the first two counts while the other foot crosses and lands outside of the sticks for the third count.
		Demonstrate steps slowly
		
		REPEAT THESE STEPS SLOWLY

	C. A third step, the turn, is basically is doing a "cross-over" twice.	
	D. The fourth step is also a "double" step, where you have both feet in between the sticks.	
Restate purpose	**CONCLUSION** I. So I hope this speech has taught you a little about the national dance of the Philippines, what things you will need for the dance, and how to do a few of the steps.	
Clincher	II. I also hope that this speech inspires you to learn more about either your heritage or one different from your own. You may be pleasantly surprised by what you discover, and you may see that you can do something this.	Do steps/dance at regular pace.

Works Cited

Alejandro, Reynaldo Gamboa, and Amanda Abad Santos-Gana. *Sayaw: Philippine Dances.* Manila, Phil.: National Bookstore, 2002.

Huber, Diane. "5,000 come to dance, honor diverse cultures." *Knight Ridder Tribune Business News* 11 February 2007, 1.

"Spotlight on the 2003 SIGTel Online Learning Award Winners." *ISTE Membership* 2003. Internet. 13 February 2007 <http://www.iste.org/Content/NavigationMenu/Membership/SIGs/SIGTel_Telelearning_/SIGTel_Online_Learning_Award/20037/Rex,_Marion.htm>.

Rose Soliven
Demonstration Speech
COMM-R110 Fundamentals of Speech Communication

Self Evaluation for Demonstration Speech

I think that I spent an adequate amount of time gathering information, preparing, and practicing for my demonstration speech. Because the topic of my speech—a Filipino folk dance called the *tinikling*—was one with which I was familiar; I had a general idea of where I could locate sources and the materials needed for the dance. I did, however, spend a good amount of time looking for newspaper articles and websites that would enhance the content of my speech. I think I spent a decent amount of time preparing my speech because after writing a draft, I recited the speech several times to determine whether I had to alter it in any way. After practicing enough to get a feel of the speech, I could have practiced more to get the speech more firmly rooted in my memory. I did practice reciting my speech both by myself and before a friend.

I think that I chose interesting information for my speech because I explained how the dance movements imitate a bird dodging bamboo traps in the rice fields. I also provided examples of how people all over the world, like Marion Rex's students in Canada, learn the dance. I feel that I creatively presented the information by dressing in traditional Filipino attire and by how I spoke. I think my tone and vocal inflections helped warm the audience to my topic.

I think that I did not use my visual aids effectively. I did not keep the photo of *tinikling* dancers on the screen for a very long time, and it probably would have been more helpful if I had shown a video clip of the dance rather than just a picture. Showing a video would have helped the audience see the dance movements in fluid motion, observe the actual speed of the dance, and hear the kind of music that accompanies the dance.

The audience probably could not do the demonstration themselves because it may be difficult to obtain the materials essential for the dance, like the long poles and music that plays at the right speed. Although I attempted to teach the basic steps, there are other conditions that need to be met to do the dance, like having people who can click the sticks in time with the music. Also, it would be difficult for the audience to reproduce the dance because they just saw me do the dance; it probably would have been more beneficial if they were able to physically try the steps as I describe how to do them.

I think that my information was appropriately organized because it followed a logical order. I began with the origins of the dance and described how the dance was used today (to showcase the Filipino culture and to be taught in schools). Next, I described the various materials needed for the dance if one wanted to perform the dance. Then, the final main point of my speech consisted of me actually demonstrating some of the dance steps.

I think I did make eye contact with the audience at times, however, not as much as I should have. I could have looked around the room and made eye contact with everyone more, instead of looking down at my note cards as often as I did. I depended on my notes for indications for every sentence.

I think that I used appropriate body language because I gestured with my hands when it seemed necessary, and I used my hands to help indicate what each leg does during the dance. It appears that I may have reduced my nervousness because I did not wring my hands like I did in my first speech. I think I could have improved my posture during the beginning of the speech because I think I stood too casually.

I think that I was understandable because I tried to speak clearly, loudly enough, and at a decent rate. Although I attempted to speak slower, I think my speaking rate still sped up. My rate is something I still need to work on because my speaking quickly could deter my audience from fully understanding me. I think I spoke enthusiastically because my vocal tone was varied and not monotonous. I think I exerted my energy and passion for the topic in the lively way I spoke.

Because my speech was 6 minutes and 45 seconds long, I did achieve the time limits because when I first wrote a draft of my speech, I recited it to see if I had to change it to fit within the time parameters. When I had practiced the speech, my time was usually around 6 minutes and 30 seconds, and so I knew that I would most likely achieve the time limits.

I used my note cards to remind me in what order my points were and what were the sub-points of my main points. I also included information about the people I quoted, in case I forgot how to attribute them. After I had practiced a few times with my outline, I practiced my speech with my note cards, since I will only have the note cards during the speech. I noticed that during my speech, I often looked down at my note cards to make sure I knew what sentence was next; however, I think I looked down at them too often. I visibly lowered my head to look at them, and so it may appear that I am paying less attention to my audience.

Some of the things I did well were speaking enthusiastically, clearly articulating my words, projecting my voice, and slowly explaining the steps of the dance. Speaking enthusiastically was effective because doing so brought energy and interest to my speech. Clearly articulating my words was effective because doing so made it easier for my audience to understand what I was saying. Projecting my voice was effective because then my audience would not have to strain to hear what I was saying. Slowly explaining the steps of the dance was effective because doing so helped the audience see what exactly was happening for each count of each dance step.

Some of the things I did that were ineffective included not using visual aids well, speaking too quickly, and depending on my notes. By not using visual aids effectively, my audience lost a visual component that could have helped them better understand how the dance went. My speaking too quickly may have prevented my audience from catching everything I said. By depending on my notes, I could not pay as much attention to the audience and make as much eye contact as I would like.

One aspect of my speeches that consistently needs improvement is my speaking rate. I plan to place a greater emphasis on slowing down when I practice speaking and designating specific places in my speech where I should pause. I will write on my note card to speak slowly.

Some of the things that I am doing better include articulating my words clearly, presenting enthusiasm in my voice, and maintaining a decent speaking volume.

THE SPEECH TO EXPLAIN

What Is a Speech to Explain and Why Is it Required?

The word "explain" is defined as "to make level or plain; to make clear or intelligible." Your ability to make a concept, process, event or object clear and understandable, even memorable, is your goal in this speech. **Your ability to make your ideas clear and understandable to your audience will define your success in all other types of speaking.**

The purpose of this speech is to explain a concept, process, event or object so that it is completely understandable to your audience (see ideas below; or your teacher will tell you his/her requirements). The emphasis is upon **understanding** and **NOT** upon doing or being able to perform a task, as in the speech to demonstrate.

The word understand is defined as "to know thoroughly; to grasp or perceive clearly." With this in mind, it is not enough for your audience to just "know about" your topic; your aim is to develop in the minds of your listeners a **thorough** understanding of your topic by using stories, comparisons, examples, illustrations, visuals, statistics, testimony, etc. that your audience can relate to.

Audience response and *expectation* in a Speech to Explain should include the following:

- This is interesting material.

- This is beneficial and relevant to my life.

- I understand this information.

- This information/process is very clear to me.

- Ah HA! Now I get it!

Insightful knowledge of your audience's interest in, level of knowledge of, and expectations with regard to your topic is crucial, as is thorough research work. *Your research work in this speech may include Internet sources.*

What Skills You Will Learn

1. You practice choosing a **topic that will interest** or benefit your audience.

2. You practice construction of a **very narrow specific purpose.**

3. You will conduct research on your speech purpose from a **variety** of sources.

   ■ You will practice **discerning credible Internet sources.**

   ■ You will discover **credible web sites and databases** related to your topic.

   ■ You will attempt to **find a researcher or expert in your topic area. (optional)**

4. You will learn to **generate visual aids using PowerPoint** or similar software

5. You will choose an **appropriate organizational structure** for your purpose.

6. You will practice using vivid descriptive language.

7. You will practice **adapting your material to your audience.**

8. You will practice **appropriate aspects of delivery.**

9. You will craft an **attention-getting introduction** and **effective conclusion.**

Sample Topics: (See Chapter 14 of Your Text for More Ideas)

Explaining a Concept
What is WARP speed?
What is Taoism?
What is psycholinguistics?
What is the Doppler Theory?

Explaining an Event
The Holocaust
Mini-meteor showers
Advent and return of Jesus
El Niño weather system

Explaining a Process
What is xerography?
How does HIV replicate itself?
How is a compact disk generated?
How does power steering work?

Explaining an Object
Digital cameras
HDTV set
Bill Gates
Scottish Rite Cathedral

What Are the Requirements for This Speech?

1. Completed **Audience Analysis/Adaptation Sheet**

2. **Topic beneficial or relevant** to your audience

3. A **narrowed, audience-centered specific purpose and central idea**

4. A typed or **word-processed preparation outline** with the following functions labeled:

   ■ Introduction and parts

   ■ Body and parts

- Conclusion and parts
- Transitions and summaries written out
- Types of support material and stylistic devices used
- Physical behaviors described in right-hand column
- Properly documented bibliography from at least **4 types of sources (periodicals, books, web sites, interview),** and cited in-text.
- **MLA format** for all sources, cited on Works Cited page, Works Consulted page (if required by your instructor), and in-text citations. See MLA guidelines in Preparation Outline section of this book
- type of organizational structure labeled

5. At least **4** completely identified **oral source citations**

6. **Design and generate at least 2 visuals using PowerPoint or similar presentational software. Please put printed copies of your slides in your speech folder and have transparencies prepared as backups in case the internet, or Oncourse fails.**

7. An **interesting, involving, appropriate introduction** and conclusion

8. Use of **three note cards** maximum—to be turned in

9. **Time minimum, 5 minutes, maximum 7 minutes**

10. **Self-evaluation** submitted by instructor's deadline.

Task Checklist (✔ Check Off as You Accomplish Them)

❏ 1. Carefully **choose a subject** that has depth and which fits the assignment well.

❏ 2. **Construct a very narrow specific purpose/central idea.**

❏ 3. **Analyze audience information;** choose target audience adaptations. (Review Lucas, Chap. 5)

❏ 4. **Research** your purpose as follows:

- Find web sites and databases which have information you can use.
- Determine the credibility/validity of the sources (see web site exercise in appendix).

Optional below:

- Discover the E-mail address/phone number **of a researcher/expert on your topic.**
- Design a "query" or formulate interview questions (See Lucas, Chap. 5).
- Conduct an E-mail or standard interview (see discussion on pages following.)

❏ 5. **Conduct research** as necessary (library, Web, etc.).

❏ 6. **Create your preparation outline.**

❏ 7. Create an attention-getting, involving **introduction and conclusion.**

❏ 8. Design and generate **at least 2 visuals from PowerPoint or similar software.** Save your visuals to RESOURCES in Oncourse CL. Bring visuals to class on a flash drive or CDROM.

❏ 9. **Practice** your speech from your preparation outline. **Time** yourself.

❏ 10. **Practice** with visuals three times! **Time** yourself. **Edit** speech if necessary.

❏ 11. **Create note cards.** *DO NOT write out your speech or preparation outline word-for-word on your note cards!* **Practice** from note cards with visuals. Time. Edit. Practice and time.

❏ 12. **Check overhead projector and other room/equipment requirements** before you speak.

❏ 13. Hand your instructor your **preparation outline, Audience Analysis/Adaptation Sheet** and 2 copies of the **Speaker Evaluation Sheet** before you speak.

❏ 14. **Review your video tape** after you have spoken. Thoughtfully write your **Self-Evaluation** and submit it to your instructor as required

Grading Criteria

Grading Criteria for this Speech: See the Speaker Evaluation form and the Outline Grading Sheet in the Coursebook. *Apply these criteria to what you have prepared in order to optimize your grade points.*

USING LIBRARY RESOURCES TO LOCATE AN EXPERT OR RESEARCHER

By Susan Schlag
Assistant Librarian
IUPUI University Library
Fall 1998

Experts are everywhere. They simplify our lives by maintaining specialized expertise in all sorts of areas—from health care to auto repair. To maintain their knowledge, these experts must remain keenly aware of trends and developments in their fields. Practicing experts—the ones we rely on for our flu vaccine or for our car's engine troubles—must themselves rely on the ultimate experts, the *researchers,* for the latest information. These researchers are those individuals actively involved in conducting experiments, lab tests, and surveys, and sharing the results of such research, to create and build new understanding. These efforts—researching and publishing—keep our everyday practitioners informed and up-to-date.

These researchers are engaged in virtually every area of inquiry imaginable. For example:

- psychologists unravel the mystery of consumer behavior—why people buy the products they buy

- meteorologists seek to understand storm system processes

- doctors test new therapies for the treatment of cancer

- sociologists explain group dynamics

- political scientists predict how voters will cast their ballots

- educators try new teaching strategies in the classroom

- linguists study differences between regional or cultural dialects

- chemists develop new household products

- engineers devise new automobile parts for increased fuel efficiency

- and so on.

Many researchers are employed as professors at colleges and universities all over the world. Besides teaching, these individuals also must "contribute to knowledge" by conducting research and writing up the results for publication in scholarly journals (or, less frequently, on the World Wide Web). Thus, researchers are usually *authors* as well. The journals in which their research is published can readily be found within most major university libraries, including IUPUI University Library—in either a traditional print or newer electronic format.

In your Speech to Explain, you must tap the knowledge of an expert or researcher via an e-mail query. Now that you understand the nature of their work, and the process by which they make their work public, finding these individuals is a straightforward, 4-step process, involving a little ingenuity and library resources that are already at your fingertips:

1. At the library, **perform some preliminary searching on your topic using an appropriate *index*.** An index is simply a list of articles—usually just the title, author, place of publication, date, and publication details—written by experts/researchers (and sometimes, other writers such as news reporters.) Indexes are available in both print and electronic formats; however, most students find electronic indexes easier to use since they can be searched by using everyday keywords such as "tornadoes" or "sales philosophy" or "cardiopulmonary resuscitation." In addition, indexes are available as either general (i.e., Expanded Academic Index) or subject-specific (i.e., PsycInfo) in scope (see the LIBRARY section for a more detailed discussion of the various indexes.) Some indexes will even present the entire article—or "full text"—directly on your computer screen. However, this is far more often the exception than the rule. If you need help, ask a librarian.

   Note: Be creative in how you think about your topic. If your topic is "buying a car," think about those who would be conducting research in this area. *Consumer Reports* regularly conducts tests on new cars; government agencies like the Department of Transportation compile statistics as well. Psychologists explore topics like persuasive communication, consumer attitudes, and sales philosophy. Try to "think out of the box" for maximum results.

2. Once you conduct your preliminary search on an appropriate index, scan your results. **Identify interesting, relevant articles—and note the *authors* of these articles.** You have just found several experts/researchers!

3. To increase your knowledge of your expert/researchers' areas of interest, obtain and read copies of specific articles relevant to you. Use INDYCAT (and perform a Journal Title Search) to determine if University Library owns a subscription to the particular journal. If so, note the call number and proceed to the stacks to retrieve the volume you need. Taking the time to review an expert/researcher's work at this point will enable you to formulate a succinct, knowledgeable query.

4. **Look up the author's e-mail address in a *directory*.** University Library provides access to several e-mail directories from its home page (*<http://www.lib.iupui.edu>*), under its Reference and Research Tools button. WhoWhere, for example, is easy-to-use. Keep searching names until you locate several whom you can query. You will likely need to query more than one expert/researcher before you obtain a suitable response. Another option is to use the National Faculty Directory (assuming that the expert/researcher is a member of a college or University faculty). This directory (REF L901 N34 v.29 1999) will help you identify the specific college or university with which the expert/researcher is affiliated. Once you know the name of the school, locating that school's home page on the World Wide Web, and individual faculty members' e-mail addresses, is fairly straightforward. Ask a librarian if you need assistance.

EXPLANATION SPEECH: AUDIENCE ANALYSIS/ADAPTATION

My Specific Purpose is:_____

My Central Idea is: _____

Directions

Analyze your audience's depth of knowledge concerning your topic. Based on your survey, explain how much your audience already knows about your topic and how much and what type of support materials you must to include so that your audience understands your topic thoroughly. Be specific. Check sample Audience Analysis in Coursebook. Base your comments on the concerns listed below and refer to your audience survey so that you are able to craft a thoughtful response. Submit as per instructor's directions.

- How much does the audience already know about my topic? How do I know this?

- If they know very little, how much and what types of support materials will I have to include in order for my audience to understand my topic thoroughly? Be specific.

- If my audience already knows a lot about my topic, what kinds of information should I include to keep their interest? Should I modify my purpose?

ASSIGNMENT #5

Explain Speech—Informative

Assignments & Scores:
- Speech _____
Outline _____
Audience Analysis _____
Self-Evaluation _____

Speaker Evaluation Sheet

I visited the Speaker's Lab for this assignment. Circle one.   YES   NO

Name _____ Section _____ Date _____

Specific Purpose and Central Idea (SP/CI) _____

_____

	Points/Score	Comments

Introduction
- Gained attention/interest   ____/____
- Revealed topic clearly (SP)   ____/____
- Showed relevance to audience   ____/____
- Established speaker credibility   ____/____
- Previewed body of speech (CI)   ____/____

Body
- Main points clearly presented   ____/____
- Points arranged in effective org. pattern   ____/____
- Points fully developed/balanced   ____/____
- Used variety of strong research material   ____/____
- Researched support material for target audience ____/____
- Used descriptive, clear, language   ____/____
- Make clear effective transitions   ____/____

Conclusion
- Prepared audience for conclusion   ____/____
- Reviewed purpose and points   ____/____
- Closed with circular construction or other device ____/____

Delivery
- Used extemporaneous style   ____/____
- Maintained eye contact with audience ____/____
- Used body and space effectively   ____/____
- Used voice effectively   ____/____
  (vol., rate, pitch, artic., voc. pauses, etc.)
- Used note cards effectively   ____/____
- Evidence of preparation and practice ____/____
- Personal enthusiasm evident   ____/____

Overall
- Maintained time parameters _____ ____/____
- Selected, prepared and used visuals effectively ____/____
- Credible sources cited effectively (4)   ____/____

* SPEECH SCORE   ____/____

ASSIGNMENT #5

Explain Speech—Informative

Speaker Evaluation Sheet

I visited the Speaker's Lab for this assignment. Circle one.   YES   NO

Name _____ Section _____ Date _____

Specific Purpose and Central Idea (SP/CI) _____

_____

	Points/Score	Comments

Introduction
- Gained attention/interest ____/____
- Revealed topic clearly (SP) ____/____
- Showed relevance to audience ____/____
- Established speaker credibility ____/____
- Previewed body of speech (CI) ____/____

Body
- Main points clearly presented ____/____
- Points arranged in effective org. pattern ____/____
- Points fully developed/balanced ____/____
- Used variety of strong research material ____/____
- Researched support material for target audience ____/____
- Used descriptive, clear, language ____/____
- Make clear effective transitions ____/____

Conclusion
- Prepared audience for conclusion ____/____
- Reviewed purpose and points ____/____
- Closed with circular construction or other device ____/____

Delivery
- Used extemporaneous style ____/____
- Maintained eye contact with audience ____/____
- Used body and space effectively ____/____
- Used voice effectively ____/____
  (vol., rate, pitch, artic., voc. pauses, etc.)
- Used note cards effectively ____/____
- Evidence of preparation and practice ____/____
- Personal enthusiasm evident ____/____

Overall
- Maintained time parameters _____ ____/____
- Selected, prepared and used visuals effectively ____/____
- Credible sources cited effectively (4) ____/____

* SPEECH SCORE ____/____

ASSIGNMENT #5

Explain Speech—Informative

Outline Grading Sheet

ATTACH THIS SHEET TO YOUR OUTLINE

Name _____ Section _____ Date _____

Criteria for grading your outline are as follows: Points/Score

Topic/Format

- ■ Chose subject appropriate to assignment   _____
- ■ Crafted clear, narrow SP and CI   _____
- ■ Used 3-column outline—word processed   _____
- ■ Proper coordination, subordination, indentation, symbolization   _____
- ■ Wrote main points and sub-points in complete sentences   _____
- ■ 4 sources (minimum) cited on Works Cited page (MLA)   _____
- ■ Note cards (Speaking outline) reflect Preparation Outline—neat   _____

Introduction

- ■ Crafted and labeled all 5 parts of introduction   _____

Body

- ■ Cited sources in-text (MLA)   _____
- ■ Chose effective organizational pattern—labeled   _____
- ■ Wrote transitions out and labeled—effective   _____
- ■ Developed main points fully and comprehensively   _____
- ■ Identified types of support material—labeled   _____
- ■ Identified types of stylistic devices—labeled   _____
- ■ Indicated physical behaviors in right column   _____
- ■ Used descriptive, clear, powerful language   _____
- ■ Stated one idea per symbol.   _____
- ■ OTHER _____   _____

Conclusion

- ■ Crafted 2-part conclusion, labeled   _____

TOTAL OUTLINE SCORE   _____

EXPLANATION SPEECH:
PEER LISTENING SHEET (1)

Speaker _____   Listener _____

Section# _____   Topic _____

A. Audience adaptation

1. How did this speaker attempt to adapt the content of the speech to this audience?

2. Provide at least one constructive suggestion for how the audience adaptation in this speech could be improved.

B. Delivery

1. Choose two ways the speaker utilized strong aspects of delivery (eye contact, volume, rate, articulation, enthusiasm, gestures, and posture).

2. What single aspect of delivery should the speaker work on before the next speech?

C. Language Clarity

1. How were ideas made clear with examples, illustrations and visuals? Cite at least one instance. If ideas were not clear or vivid, how would you suggest that the speaker modify his/her use of support materials? Cite one instance.

EXPLANATION SPEECH: PEER LISTENING SHEET (2)

Speaker _____ Listener _____

Section# _____ Topic _____

A. Audience adaptation

1. How did this speaker attempt to adapt the content of the speech to this audience?

2. Provide at least one constructive suggestion for how the audience adaptation in this speech could be improved.

B. Delivery

1. Choose two ways the speaker utilized strong aspects of delivery (eye contact, volume, rate, articulation, enthusiasm, gestures, and posture).

2. What single aspect of delivery should the speaker work on before the next speech?

C. Language Clarity

1. How were ideas made clear with examples, illustrations and visuals? Cite at least one instance. If ideas were not clear or vivid, how would you suggest that the speaker modify his/her use of support materials? Cite one instance.

EXPLANATION SPEECH: PEER LISTENING SHEET (3)

Speaker _____ Listener _____

Section# _____ Topic _____

A. Audience adaptation

1. How did this speaker attempt to adapt the content of the speech to this audience?

2. Provide at least one constructive suggestion for how the audience adaptation in this speech could be improved.

B. Delivery

1. Choose two ways the speaker utilized strong aspects of delivery (eye contact, volume, rate, articulation, enthusiasm, gestures, and posture).

2. What single aspect of delivery should the speaker work on before the next speech?

C. Language Clarity

1. How were ideas made clear with examples, illustrations and visuals? Cite at least one instance. If ideas were not clear or vivid, how would you suggest that the speaker modify his/her use of support materials? Cite one instance.

EXPLANATION SPEECH:
PEER LISTENING SHEET (4)

Speaker _____   Listener _____

Section# _____   Topic _____

A. Audience adaptation

1. How did this speaker attempt to adapt the content of the speech to this audience?

2. Provide at least one constructive suggestion for how the audience adaptation in this speech could be improved.

B. Delivery

1. Choose two ways the speaker utilized strong aspects of delivery (eye contact, volume, rate, articulation, enthusiasm, gestures, and posture).

2. What single aspect of delivery should the speaker work on before the next speech?

C. Language Clarity

1. How were ideas made clear with examples, illustrations and visuals? Cite at least one instance. If ideas were not clear or vivid, how would you suggest that the speaker modify his/her use of support materials? Cite one instance.

EXPLANATION SPEECH:
PEER LISTENING SHEET (5)

Speaker _____ Listener _____

Section# _____ Topic _____

A. Audience adaptation

1. How did this speaker attempt to adapt the content of the speech to this audience?

2. Provide at least one constructive suggestion for how the audience adaptation in this speech could be improved.

B. Delivery

1. Choose two ways the speaker utilized strong aspects of delivery (eye contact, volume, rate, articulation, enthusiasm, gestures, and posture).

2. What single aspect of delivery should the speaker work on before the next speech?

C. Language Clarity

1. How were ideas made clear with examples, illustrations and visuals? Cite at least one instance. If ideas were not clear or vivid, how would you suggest that the speaker modify his/her use of support materials? Cite one instance.

EXPLANATION SPEECH: PEER LISTENING SHEET (6)

Speaker _____   Listener _____

Section# _____   Topic _____

A. Audience adaptation

1. How did this speaker attempt to adapt the content of the speech to this audience?

2. Provide at least one constructive suggestion for how the audience adaptation in this speech could be improved.

B. Delivery

1. Choose two ways the speaker utilized strong aspects of delivery (eye contact, volume, rate, articulation, enthusiasm, gestures, and posture).

2. What single aspect of delivery should the speaker work on before the next speech?

C. Language Clarity

1. How were ideas made clear with examples, illustrations and visuals? Cite at least one instance. If ideas were not clear or vivid, how would you suggest that the speaker modify his/her use of support materials? Cite one instance.

EXPLANATION SPEECH: PEER LISTENING SHEET (7)

Speaker _____   Listener _____

Section# _____   Topic _____

A. Audience adaptation

1. How did this speaker attempt to adapt the content of the speech to this audience?

2. Provide at least one constructive suggestion for how the audience adaptation in this speech could be improved.

B. Delivery

1. Choose two ways the speaker utilized strong aspects of delivery (eye contact, volume, rate, articulation, enthusiasm, gestures, and posture).

2. What single aspect of delivery should the speaker work on before the next speech?

C. Language Clarity

1. How were ideas made clear with examples, illustrations and visuals? Cite at least one instance. If ideas were not clear or vivid, how would you suggest that the speaker modify his/her use of support materials? Cite one instance.

EXPLANATION SPEECH: SELF-EVALUATION SHEET

Directions

Review your speech from your video tape. Write a **reflective narrative** evaluating your performance and basing your comments on your thoughtful responses to the concerns and issues below. Be sure your work is typed or word-processed. See sample explain self-evaluations in the section following. Submit per instructor's directions.

- Did I spend enough time gathering information/preparing/practicing? Explain.

- Did I choose interesting information and was I creative with it? Give examples.

- Was my information clear and well developed for this audience? Why or why not?

- Is it likely the audience could effectively repeat the information themselves after hearing my speech?

- Was my information appropriately organized? Explain.

- Was my delivery appropriate (eye contact, body language, passionate attitude, articulation, enthusiasm)?

- Did I achieve the time limits? Why or why not?

- How did I use my note cards? Be specific.

- I did the following things effectively and here's why there were effective. Cite evidence from Peer Evaluations as well as teacher response from Speaker Evaluation.

- Here are the main things I did wrong and how I intend to correct them: Cite evidence from Peer Evaluations as well as teacher response from Speaker Evaluation.

- Despite everything, here are some things at which I am consistently doing better, most of the time:

THE SPEECH TO EXPLAIN

S
A
M
P
L
E

PATTI BENNETT

Audience Analysis—The Speech to Explain
Patti Bennett

The specific purpose for my speech to explain is: To inform my audience the steps to anger management. The central idea is: The steps to anger management are examining anger management skills, understanding fundamental states and forms of anger, and effective methods to anger management.

After distributing a questionnaire to my classmates about their experience with anger, I found out a lot about their what makes them angry, how they handle their anger and how it affects their loved ones. Everyone in the class experiences some degree of anger. On a scale from one (lowest) to ten (highest), the average anger for everyday life was a three. On the same scale, the average of the angriest they've ever been was an eight. Exactly half of the class said their anger affects their loved ones. There were many different reasons why they become angry. Stupidity, dishonesty, ex-husbands were just a few. The winner of the "what makes you angry" question was: bad drivers! They handle anger in many different ways. Prayer, exercise, deep breathing, yelling, and keeping it bottled up inside were mentioned.

I believe my audience knows a lot about anger. Even though I know a lot about anger too, I believe researching anger management skills, understanding fundamental states and forms of anger and effective methods to anger management; and presenting it in an organized and understandable way will help the class be more prepared next time they feel angry. There are times when I feel angry, but in the heat of my anger I don't stop to think what steps I can take to calm down. Preparing this speech will hopefully help everyone stop and think before anger gets a hold of them!

The research I've done so far is pretty basic, textbook information. (In other words, boring!) So I am thinking about some ways to make it interesting. While experimenting with the PowerPoint software, I found a clipart of a frustrated driver. I believe I'll use that in my presentation. I listen to a tape called "How to be a no-limit person" by Dr. Wayne Dyer that has a humorous excerpt of traffic and what it does to people. I may include that in my speech. I have an ex-husband and his wife who make me very angry, so I could include descriptive stories about my experience with them! Anger is a serious subject, but I hope to get my point across in a light-hearted, yet informative way.

Patti Bennett

R110

Specific Purpose: To inform my audience about three main approaches to controlling anger.

Central Idea: The three main approaches to controlling anger are expressing, suppressing and calming.

**Topical Order		
	INTRODUCTION	
Attention	I. On July 28, 2000, my ex-husband, two years after our divorce, served me with papers to sue me for custody of our children; claiming I am an unfit mother.	Eye contact with audience
Reveal Topic	II. In the last two years I have experienced many emotions, anger being the strongest. Learning to deal with anger has been essential to the welfare of my family.	
Relevancy	III. After reading the surveys I passed out last class period, I know anger touches many of us in many ways. I hope sharing my experiences will help you understand the importance of controlling anger.	Don't fidget.
Credibility	IV. Through family counseling and much research, I have found ways to help control anger. It's not easy, but it's worth the time and effort.	
Preview	V. The National Mental Health Association states there are "three main approaches to controlling anger: expressing, suppressing and calming." Let's look at each approach. (National… p.2)	
**Internal preview		
	BODY	
Main Point Sub Point	I. One way to control anger is to express your feelings.	Show transparency
	A. Learning how to vent constructively is a way to express anger. According to Clayton Tucker-Ladd, author of the book Psychological self-help on the web "healthy, effective venting will probably involve exhaustion, i.e. vigorously expressing the feelings until you are drained." (Tucker…p.2)	
	1. Running around the block would be an example.	
	2. Using a punching bag would be another example.	
	B. In my family, when tensions are mounting, we dance.	Show enthusiasm
**Brief example	1. We put a CD with sixties music into the CD player.	
	2. We dance until we can't dance any more!	

TRANSITION ****Parallelism**	Someday, when my children are grown and gone, I hope it's the dancing they will remember, not the anger. Now let's look at suppressing anger in a healthy way.	

Main Point
 	
Sub Point
 	
**Extended
    example
	II. Another way to control anger is to suppress it and use the energy in a positive way.
	    A. Dr. George Rhoades, a psychotherapist and author, who developed an anger management program, says "We need to learn how to have humor in our lives." (Rhoades...p. 2)
	        1. Hopefully, you experienced how laughter is contagious.
	        2. Laughter is a gift, don't be afraid to use it.
	    B. I want to tell you about an anger turned into laughter experience I had with my children.
	        1. We were at Chuckie Cheeses in Fort Wayne and I was suppose to follow my brother-in-law to his sister's house.
	        2. I could have been angry because I wasted time and gas money following the wrong car, but I saw the humor in the situation and started laughing uncontrollably!
		Show transparency
		
		Play audio tape
		
		Maintain eye contact

TRANSITION ****Parallelism** ****Internal** **Summary**	Someday, when my children are grown and gone, I hope it's the laughter they remember, not the anger. Expressing and suppressing are two of the ways to control anger, now lets look at calming.	

Main Point
 	
Sub Point
 	
**Brief
    example
 	
**Parallelism
	III. Another way to express anger is to calm yourself down.
	    A. The American Psychological Association recommends "relaxation" as a strategy to keep anger at bay. (American...p.4)
	        1. Deep breathing is a good way to calm down.
	        2. Visualizing a calm, relaxing experience can help calm you down.
	    B. When my children start fighting in the car, I make them calm down and say something nice about everyone in the car.
	        1. If they try to be funny and say something rude, I make them say two nice things about the person.
	        2. By the time we get to where we are going, we are calmed down and usually laughing.
	
	Someday, when my children are grown and gone, I hope it's the positive affirmations they remember, not the anger.
		Use hands to demonstrate
		
		Show transparency

Review	**CONCLUSION**	Exhibit sincerity
	I. Take it from me, anger hurts. Sometimes I cannot believe how so much anger got into my life. Anger management has taught me that life is too short to be angry. So express your anger by dancing, and suppress your anger by laughing and calm yourself down by relaxing and thinking positive thoughts!	
Clincher	II. No, I'm not a perfect mother. But I am a mother that dances and laughs and says positive things, and that can't be all bad!	SMILE!

Works Cited

American Psychological Association. "Controlling Anger, Before It Controls You." <http://www.apa.org/pubinfo/anger.html>. 6 March 2002.

National Mental Health Association. "NMHA MHIC Factsheet: General Mental Issues." http://www.nmha.org/infoctr/factsheets/44.cfm. 17 March 2002.

Rhoades, Dr. George. "Anger Management for Uncontrollable Anger, Explosive Rage." <http://www.healthyplace.com/Communities/Abuse/Site/transcripts/anger_management.htm.> 10 March 2002.

Tucker-Ladd, Clayton. "Psychological Self-Help." http://www.mentalhealth.net/psyhelp/ 6 March 2002.

Self-evaluation: Speech to Explain
Patti Bennett
R110

In my speech to explain, I spent a lot of time researching, preparing and practicing. When I did my research, I found a lot of different type of information. For instance, I found the audio I used in my speech from a website called teehee.com when I was researching about humor! I used the speakers' lab, which helped me in my preparation. I tried not to practice as much so it wouldn't sound like I memorized the speech, but I wanted to be confident in the knowledge and what I wanted to say, so I practiced in a different way. When I was at the speakers' lab, I videotaped my speech twice, so I watched the tape over and over again. I also audiotaped my speech so I could hear how I sounded.

I tried to make it an interesting speech by adding personal information to get my point across. I also believe the transition "when my children are grown and gone . . ." helped sum up my main points in a creative way. The audio with the laughter was used to lighten up the seriousness of the speech. I used simple language to make the information clear to the audience. To develop and organize the speech; I pointed out the main topic, gave examples from the research, then gave personal examples to make it understandable. I believe the personal examples and the repetition of the "when my children are grown and gone . . ." transition will make the speech memorable to the audience.

My delivery is pretty good. I believe I have good eye contact, rate, volume, and articulation. Many of my peers mentioned my gestures were strong and helped in making my point. I still believe I look as nervous as I feel (even though I exiperienced a lot less nervousness this time because I utilized the speakers' lab). I am so concerned about getting the information to the audience in an organized and understandable way, that I am less passionate or enthusiastic as I really am. With more experience in giving speeches, I will become more confident in my overall delivery and be able to show more passion and enthusiasm!

I was within the time limits since I kept the information brief. I used my note cards to help guide me through the speech. Usually one main word would remind me of what I wanted to say. I also put the cited information on them so I wouldn't misquote the source. During the last speech I forgot to put up one of my transparencies, so I used my note cards to remind me when to use my visual aids.

I effectively organized my speech, which made it flow smoothly. I was creative by using personal examples to back up the information, and by repeating what I thought was the most important message of my speech. My visual aids were simple, but got the message across without taking away from the speech. My goal is not to bore the audience with information they'll never remember. When I listen to speakers, I find the most effective speakers use real life situations to hold the audiences attention and get the message across.

I guess I used persuasive tactics without knowing it! After studying the next few chapters and giving a speech on persuasion, I'll be able to recognize what I did! I also feel my nervousness still affects my delivery, so I will use the speakers lab again and I'll go one step further by getting a mentor to evaluate my speech while I'm there!

One thing I am doing better is relieving some of my nervousness by using the speakers lab to help me. I am also learning how to narrow a topic down to find the important information to share with the audience. I also tend to have little nervous habits while speaking, so I am working to eliminate those! For example, during my first speech, one classmate told me I put my hair behind my ears, which was distracting to her. So for the second speech I put my hair in combs so I wouldn't unconsciously be concerned with it!

PERSUASIVE
UNIT

The Need Step Argument
The Speech to Persuade on a Question of Policy
Monroe's Motivated Sequence Audience Response
and Speaker Tasks

PERSUASION UNIT RATIONALE

What Are Persuasive Speeches and Why Are They Required?

Whereas the purpose of information in informational speaking is to create understanding, the purpose of information in persuasive speaking is to initiate change.

■ In informational speaking, ideas are offered for consumption only and the speaker's general purpose usually does not include an intention to influence thinking or behavior.

■ In persuasive speaking, the speaker selects specific, audience-related information to inspire change. Change implies movement from one position, attitude, belief or behavior to another. The movement can be mental (speeches to convince, to inspire, the one-point) or physical (speeches to actuate, motivate).

Audience expectations, when listening to persuasive speeches are

■ that the speaker will give logical, credible, and relevant reasons for change,

■ that these reasons be put into a logical framework(argument),

■ that they perceive that the speaker believes what he/she is saying.

Chapter 15 of your text describes the many times during your day that you are placed in a position where it is necessary for you to "change" someone's way of thinking or behavior. The two speeches in this unit offer you the opportunity to attempt to influence the behavior of your classmates in the One-Point Persuasive and Persuasive Speech of Policy.

The **Need Step Argument** is provided to introduce you to the concept of learning to support a statement or claim with good reasons backed up with solid evidence. This assertion/support strategy is central to all good persuasive speaking and will help you to create the argument that a problem exists and is serious for your Policy Speech.

In a **Persuasive Speech on a Question of Policy** you will attempt to move your audience to *behave* differently. For example, if you are attempting to motivate your audience to sign their licenses and become organ donors, you must use a combination of strategies appropriate to the beliefs and attitudes of your target audience. Before people act differently, they must be convinced mentally and emotionally that there is a problem, that it is serious and that it affects them (your Need Step Argument). You must also make them uncomfortable enough about the problem to cause them to feel like acting, hopefully to support the course of action you have proposed (your specific purpose). Therefore, this last speech will be a combination of all your have learned thus far (be sure to read Ch. 15 and 16 of your textbook).

In both of these assignments you will be practicing "real life" skills. If you are not "convinced" of this yet, **do the journaling assignment at the end of Chapter 15** of your text under "Exercises For Critical Thinking." Keeping a journal for a day regarding your communication experiences may be enough to "persuade" you that unit is, indeed, a most necessary, challenging and important set of assignments.

THE NEED STEP ARGUMENT

What is the Need Step Argument?

Assignment #6, the Need Step Argument, will help you prepare for your last speech, the persuasive Speech of Policy (Speaking Assignment #7.) The Need Step Argument is a short speech that will help you become aware of the persuasive concepts of **assertion (reasons) and support (evidence)** as well as to assist you in completing the Need Step for the *Speech to Persuade on a Question Of Policy* (Policy Speech.)

The Need Step in the Policy Speech is the part of the speech that proves that there is a PROBLEM or NEED, that the NEED is serious and affects your audience directly or indirectly. Once you have completed Speech #6 (Need Step Argument), you will be well on your way to finishing your final Speech #7 (Policy Speech.)

> **To prepare for Assignment #6, The Need Step Argument, you must pick a topic and create a Specific Purpose for Assignment #7, the Policy Speech. Please read Speaking Assignment #7, in your *R110 Coursebook* (The Policy Speech) NOW. Identify a problem that you are passionate about and create a Specific Purpose, confirming it with your instructor.**

Then, please read Chapter 15 of your text and pay close attention to Dr. Lucas's discussion of the Monroe Motivated Sequence. In order to accomplish Speaking Assignment #6, The Need Step Argument, you must understand the parts of the Monroe Motivated Sequence, which is a pattern for organizing a persuasive speech. You are required to use this organizational pattern for Speaking Assignment #7, the Policy Speech. Speaking Assignment #6 will help you to create a portion of the Monroe Sequence, called the NEED STEP. The NEED STEP is the part of a persuasive speech that makes your audience feel the NEED for a change. This is where you must argue that the problem you identified exists, is serious, won't go away, and relates directly or indirectly to the audience. Here is where you make your audience FEEL so uncomfortable that they want to help solve the problem!

If you have read about the Speech Of Policy in your R110 Coursebook and you have read Chapter 15 in your textbook, then do this:

First

Pick a problem that you feel really, really passionate about. (This will be your problem for the Policy Speech.)

Here are some examples of problems:

- There is a shortage of usable blood
- There are inadequate immigration laws
- Drivers cause accidents while using cell phones
- **There is too much traffic on Indianapolis roads**
- There is not enough research money for breast cancer

Second

Draft a specific purpose for the Policy Speech #7. (Make sure you draft a purpose that states exactly what *action* you want your audience to take.)

Here are some examples of Specific Purposes based on the problems above:

- To persuade my audience *to donate* blood regularly.
- To persuade my audience *to petition* their representatives for stricter immigration laws.
- To motivate the R110 class *not to talk* on cell phones while driving.
- **To persuade the R110 class *to petition* our state lawmakers to create a regional mass transit system.**
- To motivate the students in my class *to donate time and money* to the Susan B. Komen Breast Cancer Foundation.

Third

State your CLAIM. This is a statement that indicates your position on the issue or problem you have chosen.

Here are some examples of Claims based on the Specific Purposes above:

- The need for blood is greater than the current supply.
- Current immigration laws are detrimental to the US economy.
- Drivers who talk on cell phones while driving cause traffic accidents.
- **The amount of traffic in Indianapolis is a threat to air quality and quality of life.**
- There is not enough research money to find a cure for breast cancer.

Fourth

Find out, through research, the reasons (assertions) why your claim is true. State those reasons (you must have at least three).

Example

If this is your problem: There is too much traffic on Indianapolis roads

If this is your Specific Purpose: To persuade the R110 class *to petition* our state lawmakers to create a regional mass transit system.

If this is your position or Claim: The amount of traffic in Indianapolis is a threat to air quality and quality of life. (.... because why? How?)

Then these might be your reasons (assertions): (because....?)

1. Too much traffic causes the air quality to decrease.

2. Too much traffic causes serious health issues.

3. Too much traffic affects economic development.

Fifth

Support your reasons (assertions) with credible evidence (facts, statistics, opinions) that argues that your problem is serious and worth solving. You must have at least 2 pieces of evidence for each assertion. (see sample materials below, table and outline, following.)

So, if these are your reasons (assertions) then your evidence might be:

1. Too much traffic causes the air quality to decrease. (....because......)
    a. According to the Knozone website, sponsored by the Marion Cty. Health Dept, sources that contribute to the formation of smog include emissions from automobiles, small engines (like lawnmowers) and large industry and fuel combustion sources. (Knozone)
    b. According to the US Environmental Protection Agency, the air quality Central Indiana does not meet federal health-based standards for ground-level ozone (smog) and, more recently, for fine particles (soot). (EPA)

2. Too much traffic causes serious health issues. (....because....)
    a. According to the U.S. Environmental Protection Agency, roughly one out of every three people in the United States is at a higher risk of experiencing problems from ground-level ozone. (EPA)
    b. Smog can damage a person's lungs, trigger and intensify asthma attacks and aggravate other breathing conditions. (EPA)
    c. There is also evidence that ground-level ozone can lower resistance to respiratory illnesses and chronic lung diseases, such as pneumonia, emphysema, asthma and bronchitis. (EPA)

3. Too much traffic affects economic development. (....because....)
    a. Central Indiana does not meet federal health-based standards for ground-level ozone (smog) and, more recently, for fine particles (soot). (Knozone)
    b. Clean air helps to spur economic development because without it, federal law requires the imposition of strict pollution control regulations on a region making it difficult for business and industry to expand or even relocate. (Knozone)

Since you are asking your audience to take immediate action (let's get a regional mass transportation system going!), they must be made to feel an intense NEED in order to become involved in the solution. Does the above list of reasons (assertions) and evidence, begin to create a need for mass transit? Can you find additional reasons to make this argument more compelling? Can you prove this problem is so serious that we all want to do something about it?

In order for people to take action, your argument must be a compelling one that proves the existence, seriousness and relevance of the problem. That is why we focus on the argument in this fourth speech, **The Need Step Argument, or Speaking Assignment #6 in your Coursebook.**

How is this beneficial for you?

Have you ever been at a social gathering, or professional meeting and someone asks you why you feel or believe the way you do about a certain issue or problem? Have you ever had to persuade someone to do something they didn't want to do?

Did you have your argument ready? Were your reasons based on more than just your own personal opinion or feeling? Did other people with more experience agree with your reasoning and evidence? Had you read the latest cutting-edge literature and taken your reasoning from it? Were your reasons logical? Or, did your argument amount to a "I feel this way or that way, or he-said, she-said" with little credible information?

Throughout your life there will always be people who will be asking you to tell them why you think, feel or believe the way you do. You will also have numerous opportunities to persuade people to think or act differently. In these situations, you will have to be ready with good, solid reasons (and reasoning) to "prove" whatever points you are trying to make. In many cases, your ability to support the way you believe, think or feel may make the difference between a great career and a mediocre one; an "A" in speech class or a "C"; a great date or no date at all!

What skills you will learn.

1. You will learn to choose a problem about which you feel strongly and can be made relevant to the audience. This should be your topic for Speaking Assignment #7, the Policy Speech.

2. You will learn to fashion this problem into a **Specific Purpose**, which states exactly what physical response or action you want from your audience. (The Policy speech is a speech of actuation or motivation that requires that your audience DO something, as opposed to just THINKING a certain way. See Speaking Assignment #7 for details.)

3. You will learn to define the **problem**, which gave rise to your Specific Purpose.

4. You will learn to **state your position about the problem in one complete sentence (claim).**

5. You will do research to discover at least three main reasons (**assertions**) which will support the existence, the seriousness, the inevitability and the relevancy of your problem, and which will make your audience feel uncomfortable enough to want to take action.

6. You will do further research and **uncover selective evidence** that supports your reasons with a balance of logos, ethos, and pathos.

7. You will use this evidence in a reasoned argument.

What are the Requirements for this Speech?

1. An **appropriate, researchable problem** that has two arguable sides. Check with your instructor if you are not sure. Problems where your audience is in total agreement about the action you want them to take are probably not appropriate.

2. A clearly worded **claim** (problem statement)

3. A simple audience **survey and analysis** that will reveal how strongly your audience agrees or disagrees with your claim (see Audience Analysis Adaptation, pages following), and how likely they are to follow your request for action.

4. At least **three assertions** that support your claim

5. At least **2 pieces of evidence** to support each assertion; **evidence types labeled**

6. An abbreviated **preparation outline** similar to the examples

    a. Typed or word-processed

    b. Labeled like samples in section following

    c. Works Cited page and Works Consulted page (if required by your instructor)

7. At least **3 different sources**, cited in-text (see samples) and on your Works Cited page.

8. No more than **2 note cards** (to be turned in).

9. Speak at least 2 minutes but not more than 3 minutes

10. Review your videotape and return a **self-evaluation** per instructor's deadline

Task Checklist (✔ check off as you complete each one)

❏ 1. Read requirements for Speech of Policy in the *Student Coursebook.*

❏ 2. Read Chapter 15. Note discussion about Monroe's Sequence, Need Step.

❏ 3. Choose a **problem** you feel strongly about that is researchable and arguable.

❏ 4. Draft your Specific Purpose Statement (what do you want your audience to DO?) See discussion on Speeches to Gain Immediate Action, sample SPs, page 413 in your textbook.

❏ 5. Construct your **claim** or position statement.

❏ 6. Use the survey instrument suggested in the **Audience Analysis/Adaptation** (or by your instructor) and conduct a poll of your audience.

❏ 7. **Research** your claim and choose the most effective reasons and evidence that will support it.

❏ 8. Create your **preparation outline**, making sure to **cite your sources in-text**.

❏ 9. **Practice** your speech from the preparation outline. **Ask for help** or review by a Speaker's Lab mentor.

❑ 10. Prepare a **speaking outline (Ch.10)** on your note cards. *DO NOT* write your speech or preparation outline word-for-word on your note cards! Practice, using the cards. Time yourself.

❑ 11. **Practice again** and edit cards if necessary. Check your time.

❑ 12. When it is your turn to speak, give your instructor your **outline** with **Outline Grading Sheet** attached, your **audience analysis/adaptation**, and both copies of your **Speaker Evaluation Sheet**.

❑ 13. View your videotape. Thoughtfully complete your **self-evaluation** and submit to instructor by deadline.

Grading Criteria

Grading criteria for the Speech: See the Speaker Evaluation Form and the Outline Grading Sheet in the Coursebook. *Apply these criteria to what you have prepared in order to optimize your grade points.*

Here is another example of a simplified outline of a basic argument that a problem exists and is serious. Although it could use more pathos to make it more effective, you can see how the evidence support the assertions; the assertions support the Claim, how the Claim is an aspect of the Problem, and how the Problem inspired the Specific Purpose. *Your* outline will be longer and more detailed. ONE OTHER SAMPLE APPEARS AT THE END OF THIS SECTION.

Problem

More people are killed each year with handguns than by any other means. (**Note: this is the root problem. The speaker then goes on to prove that this problem exists, and is serious. There is evidence here that makes it local, hence relevant to the lives of the audience.**)

Specific Purpose For Speech #7

To persuade the R110 class **to petition** their legislators in favor of legislation that bans the ownership of handguns. (**Note that the desired response here is that the class DO something or ACT a certain way.**)

Claim

Possession of handguns is dangerous for private citizens. (because....) (**A Claim is a position or problem statement that can be argued because it is controversial and has two sides. It forms the core of your NEED STEP. A position statement or argument needs to have reasons to support it. (Because .....WHY?)**

Assertion: (reason)   I. More people are killed *deliberately* by guns than any other weapon.

Evidence: (logos)   A. Statistical Abstracts states that 87% of all murders are performed with handguns. (*Abstracts 237*)

Evidence: (ethos/logos)   B. Edwin Dorr's book *The Life Forsaken* says that 72% of all suicides are done with handguns. (*Dorr 44*)

Assertion:(reason)   II. More people are killed *accidentally* with handguns than with any other weapon.

Evidence (logos)   A. *The New York Times* of 27 March 1995 said that guns are involved in a majority of the accidental deaths reported in 1994. (*NY Times 7*)

Evidence: (ethos)   B. Indianapolis police officer Herman Cannon told me in an interview that more accidental deaths, other than automobile accidents, were caused by guns than by any other means. (Cannon interview)

(Note the consistent use of logos, which is fact, opinion or anything that is empirically verifiable. Note also the evidence above that comes from a credible source, hence the ethos label. Had the speaker included evidence such as a case study or extended example about someone who was shot or killed, it would have personalized this argument and added pathos, which is evidence that causes people to have emotional response to a topic.)

Restatement of Claim: Therefore, I ask you to agree with me, that for these reasons, the possession of all types of handguns is dangerous for private citizens. (***This is simply a formality that summarizes your argument.***)

Here are more examples of Problems/Specific Purposes/ Claims:

Problem	Specific Purpose	Need Step CLAIM
Our food is grown with too many pesticides and herbicides.	To persuade the R110 class to purchase and consume organically grown foods.	Inorganically grown foods are hazardous to your health.
Breathing smoke is harmful to your health.	To persuade the R110 class to lobby their legislators to ban smoking in all public places in Indiana.	Secondhand smoke contains chemicals that can cause cancer in humans.
People die or are hurt needlessly because they don't wear their seatbelts.	To persuade the R110 class to wear their seatbelts while driving and to require their passengers to do the same.	More unbelted passengers die in traffic accidents that those who wear seatbelts.
Students in public schools are being needlessly harmed because of what they wear to school.	To persuade the R110 class to lobby their school representatives to require school uniforms.	Schools not requiring uniform student apparel experience more violence.

SEE A SAMPLE STUDENT NEED STEP ARGUMENT OUTLINE AT THE END OF THIS SECTION.

THE NEED STEP ARGUMENT AUDIENCE ANALYSIS/ADAPTATION

Directions

Conduct a simple poll of your audience as to their beliefs and feelings regarding your topic. Also, your teacher may allow you to use Oncourse to survey your classmates. Please check with your teacher to determine what is preferable. Hand your poll to your classmates on separate sheets of paper. Analyze your results (See Lucas, Chap. 5). What can you infer regarding the disposition of your classmates toward your topic? How will you adapt to their feelings, beliefs or attitudes? Write this out in narrative form based on the questions asked below.

My claim is: _____

_____

Conduct a simple survey (your instructor may require additional questions) using this semantic differential:

Audience responses:

1	2	3	4	5	6
Strongly Agree	Moderate Agreement	Weakly Agree	Weakly Disagree	Moderate Disagreement	Strongly Disagree

You may want to ask WHY your classmates hold whatever feelings they do and incorporate this into your analysis.

ANALYSIS

1. What were the statistical results of your survey?

2. If you discovered any additional reasons for why your audience holds a specific belief or attitude, what are they?

3. What inferences can you make from this information?

ADAPTATION

1. How will the above analysis help you to select your reasons and evidence? Did you have to do anything differently based on the above. If so, what was it? Be specific.

ASSIGNMENT #6

Need Step Argument—Persuasive

Assignments & Scores:	
•Speech	_____
Outline	_____
Audience Analysis	_____
Self-Evaluation	_____

Speaker Evaluation Sheet

I visited the Speaker's Lab for this assignment. Circle one. YES NO

Name _____ Section _____ Date _____

Claim _____

_____

	Points/Score	Comments

Introduction
■ Made brief opening statement containing Claim ____/____

Body
■ Used sufficient number of assertions ____/____
■ Used assertions that clearly support Claim ____/____
■ Chose strong, relevant evidence to
back assertions ____/____
■ Used sufficient evidence ____/____
■ Used balanced selection of logos, ethos, pathos ____/____
■ Evidence reflects audience beliefs/attitudes ____/____
■ Sufficient number of sources cited effectively ____/____

Conclusion
■ Signaled end ____/____
■ Restated claim ____/____

Delivery
■ Used extemporaneous style ____/____
■ Maintained eye contact ____/____
■ Used powerful/convincing language ____/____
■ Used voice effectively ____/____
(vol., rate, artic., voc. pauses, etc.)
■ Used body language and space effectively ____/____
■ Used note cards effectively ____/____

Overall
■ Maintained time parameters _____ ____/____

* SPEECH SCORE ____/____

ASSIGNMENT #6

Need Step Argument—Persuasive

Assignments & Scores:
• Speech _____
Outline _____
Audience Analysis _____
Self-Evaluation _____

Speaker Evaluation Sheet

I visited the Speaker's Lab for this assignment. Circle one.   YES   NO

Name _____   Section _____   Date _____

Claim _____

_____

	Points/Score	Comments

Introduction
- Made brief opening statement containing Claim   ____/____

Body
- Used sufficient number of assertions   ____/____
- Used assertions that clearly support Claim   ____/____
- Chose strong, relevant evidence to back assertions   ____/____
- Used sufficient evidence   ____/____
- Used balanced selection of logos, ethos, pathos   ____/____
- Evidence reflects audience beliefs/attitudes   ____/____
- Sufficient number of sources cited effectively   ____/____

Conclusion
- Signaled end   ____/____
- Restated claim   ____/____

Delivery
- Used extemporaneous style   ____/____
- Maintained eye contact   ____/____
- Used powerful/convincing language   ____/____
- Used voice effectively (vol., rate, artic., voc. pauses, etc.)   ____/____
- Used body language and space effectively   ____/____
- Used note cards effectively   ____/____

Overall
- Maintained time parameters _____   ____/____

* SPEECH SCORE   ____/____

ASSIGNMENT #6

Need Step Argument—Persuasive

Outline Grading Sheet

ATTACH THIS SHEET TO YOUR OUTLINE

Name _____ **Section** _____ **Date** _____

Criteria for grading your outline are as follows: Points/Score

Topic/Format

- Chose controversial (2-sided) claim, appropriate for assignment   _____
- Followed abbreviated outline format in Coursebook   _____
- Wrote assertions and support in complete sentences   _____
- Researched 3 different sources (minimum); cited on Works Cited page   _____

Introduction

- Crafted short statement of claim   _____
- Or, as assigned by instructor _____   _____

Body

- Labeled claim, assertions, and types of evidence   _____
- Cited all sources in-text (MLA)   _____
- Used sufficient number of assertions and support   _____
- Stated one idea/fact per symbol.   _____

Conclusion

- Restated claim   _____
- Or, as per instructor _____   _____

Over-all

- Word-processed, neat   _____
- Note card reflects preparation outline   _____

TOTAL OUTLINE SCORE   _____

NEED STEP ARGUMENT:
PEER LISTENING SHEET (1)

Speaker _____ Listener _____

Claim _____

A. Delivery

1. Give examples of convincing language and delivery exhibited by the speaker.

B. Argument

1. What were the major reasons the speaker gave to support his/her claim?

2. Was the supporting evidence sufficient? Was it credible? How could you tell?

3. Did the speaker create cognitive dissonance? How?

4. Based on evidence and delivery, did you experience a change in your beliefs or attitudes or feelings toward the speaker's claim? Why or why not?

NEED STEP ARGUMENT:
PEER LISTENING SHEET (2)

Speaker _____ Listener _____

Claim _____

A. Delivery

1. Give examples of convincing language and delivery exhibited by the speaker.

B. Argument

1. What were the major reasons the speaker gave to support his/her claim?

2. Was the supporting evidence sufficient? Was it credible? How could you tell?

3. Did the speaker create cognitive dissonance? How?

4. Based on evidence and delivery, did you experience a change in your beliefs or attitudes or feelings toward the speaker's claim? Why or why not?

Need Step Argument: Peer Listening Sheet (3)

Speaker _____   Listener _____

Claim _____

A. Delivery

1. Give examples of convincing language and delivery exhibited by the speaker.

B. Argument

1. What were the major reasons the speaker gave to support his/her claim?

2. Was the supporting evidence sufficient? Was it credible? How could you tell?

3. Did the speaker create cognitive dissonance? How?

4. Based on evidence and delivery, did you experience a change in your beliefs or attitudes or feelings toward the speaker's claim? Why or why not?

NEED STEP ARGUMENT:
PEER LISTENING SHEET (4)

Speaker _____ Listener _____

Claim _____

A. Delivery

1. Give examples of convincing language and delivery exhibited by the speaker.

B. Argument

1. What were the major reasons the speaker gave to support his/her claim?

2. Was the supporting evidence sufficient? Was it credible? How could you tell?

3. Did the speaker create cognitive dissonance? How?

4. Based on evidence and delivery, did you experience a change in your beliefs or attitudes or feelings toward the speaker's claim? Why or why not?

NEED STEP ARGUMENT:
PEER LISTENING SHEET (5)

Speaker _____ Listener _____

Claim _____

A. Delivery

1. Give examples of convincing language and delivery exhibited by the speaker.

B. Argument

1. What were the major reasons the speaker gave to support his/her claim?

2. Was the supporting evidence sufficient? Was it credible? How could you tell?

3. Did the speaker create cognitive dissonance? How?

4. Based on evidence and delivery, did you experience a change in your beliefs or attitudes or feelings toward the speaker's claim? Why or why not?

NEED STEP ARGUMENT:
PEER LISTENING SHEET (6)

Speaker _____ Listener _____

Claim _____

A. Delivery

1. Give examples of convincing language and delivery exhibited by the speaker.

B. Argument

1. What were the major reasons the speaker gave to support his/her claim?

2. Was the supporting evidence sufficient? Was it credible? How could you tell?

3. Did the speaker create cognitive dissonance? How?

4. Based on evidence and delivery, did you experience a change in your beliefs or attitudes or feelings toward the speaker's claim? Why or why not?

Need Step Argument:
Peer Listening Sheet (7)

Speaker _____ Listener _____

Claim _____

A. Delivery

1. Give examples of convincing language and delivery exhibited by the speaker.

B. Argument

1. What were the major reasons the speaker gave to support his/her claim?

2. Was the supporting evidence sufficient? Was it credible? How could you tell?

3. Did the speaker create cognitive dissonance? How?

4. Based on evidence and delivery, did you experience a change in your beliefs or attitudes or feelings toward the speaker's claim? Why or why not?

THE NEED STEP ARGUMENT: SELF-EVALUATION SHEET

Directions

Review your speech from your video tape. Write a **reflective narrative** evaluating your performance based on the questions below. Cite evidence from your peer and instructor evaluations. Be sure your work is typed or word-processed. See sample one-point self-evaluations in the following section.

- Did you spend enough time uncovering the most effective evidence to support your claim? Give reasons why or why not, and relate your answer to your audience analysis.

- Did you use your evidence ethically? Why or why not?

- Were your assertions and support logical? Why or why not?

- Did you show persuasive body language or use persuasive language? If so, cite examples. If not, give suggestions.

- How are you doing with your use of note cards? Have you made any improvement in your extemporaneous style? Explain.

- How successful were you in achieving the time parameters? If you were successful, tell why. If not, tell why not.

- State what you did effectively and how you could tell that you were effective.

- State the things you still have problems with and **HOW** you intend to solve them.

The Need Step Argument

Need Step Argument Materials

Survey Results for Need Step Argument
Reagan LaCour
Section 2651
13 students responded

Have you been a victim of domestic violence?
9-no, 4-yes

How about your parents? Family? Friends?
4-no, 9-yes

If you were a victim, where did you turn to for help?
9-n/a, 1-no where, 3-friends & family

If someone else, where did they go?
4-n/a, 3-friends & family, 3-divorce, 1-police, 1-army, 1-no where

Have you ever volunteered at abuse shelters? Why or why not?
11-no, 2-yes
Why?-for school, likes to volunteer
Why not?-never considered it, not well enough informed

Have you ever donated money to abuse shelters? Why or why not?
8-no, 5-yes
Why not? - never considered, not well enough informed, not enough money

If not-what would make you more inclined to do so?
1-no response, 4-n/a, 7-more info, 1-if knew someone personally

If you have-what would make you do so again?
1-more time, 1-knowing benefit shelter, 1-its the right thing to do, 1-thought of what would happen otherwise

Audience Analysis/Need Step
Reagan LaCour
Section 2651

My Claim is: There are inadequate resources and assistance for victims of domestic abuse.

Analysis

Based on the results of my student surveys, I found that 70% of the students were either close to a victim or a victim themselves, of domestic violence. The importance of this claim is to assure my audience that domestic violence is extremely prevalent in the United States. Many people believe that as a victim they are alone, while many non-victims are not aware that domestic abuse occurs so often and in amongst all classes, cultures, races and socioeconomic statuses. Of the victims that fled the abuse, many turned to friends and family for shelter. No one that fled the abuse turned to shelters for refuge. In retrospect, I would like to have asked the students why they did not consider going to a shelter as an option.

Another area that I focused my survey on was how many students contributed to battered women's shelters, either through donations or volunteering. 85% of the students had never volunteered at a shelter because they had not ever considered it or were not well-enough informed. On the other hand, 62% of those surveyed stated that they had never donated money to abuse shelter because they had also never considered it, were not well-enough informed or did not have enough money. Of the percentage of students that had never donated to abuse shelters, 85% of them said that they would be more inclined to do so if they were more informed about the cause.

Adaptation

I found that the information obtained in my surveys will prove to be very useful in my speech. First of all, because many of the students have been affected by domestic violence, I can be assured that the topic will be interesting and informative for the students. Secondly, even though the statistics state that domestic violence is a serious issue in our country, I was surprised at how many people in my class were directly affected. It is important that I use this information to relate the subject to my audience. I will need to give several statistics and examples both from the surveys and outside resources to prove these findings to be true. Many students stated that when they fled abuse or those close to them fled abuse, they found protection with family or friends. However, other resources state that many victims do not turn to friends or family for shelter because they either do not have any or are ashamed of their circumstances. This fact shows how important domestic violence shelters are to victims.

Another way to adapt the speech to my audience is to discuss the different ways to help domestic violence shelters through volunteering and donations. I need to address the reasons that students have not contributed in the past and show how to change those factors in the future. Whether their concerns are due to time or money, I need to explain how to use the resources they do have to help the shelters.

All of these areas will be useful for providing the students with information regarding abuse shelters—what they represent, who they help, how they help, what their needs are and how easy it is to make a difference. The number one reason stated for why students had not contributed in the past was due to a lack of knowledge and information. The main idea of my speech will be to inform the students so that they have the tools and the knowledge to take action in the future.

Reagan La Cour
Need Step Argument
R110—2651

Need Step Outline

Claim/Problem Statement: There are inadequate resources and assistance available for victims of domestic violence.

Assertion 1:
 	
Evidence Logos
 	
Evidence Logos
 	
Evidence Logos
 	
Evidence Pathos
	I. Domestic violence is a serious issue facing women in the United States today.
	    A. According to a recent study, domestic violence is the primary cause of injury to women between the ages of 15 and 44-more than auto accidents, muggings and rapes combined. (Trauma)
	    B. In Marion County, nearly 21,000 women are victims of domestic abuse each year. (Trauma)
	    C. As a result of my R110 class study, I found that of the 13 students that responded to my survey, 9 were either victims of domestic abuse or were close to a victim, this was a startling 70%. (Class survey)
	    D. Domestic abuse is making victims of our mothers, our sisters, our friends and even ourselves. It holds no ethnic or socioeconomic prejudice. People of African, European, Hispanic or Asian origin, rich or poor, college graduates or dropouts are all affected and at risk.

Transition	Now that I have told you about the prevalence and seriousness of domestic violence in the United States, let me tell you about the lack of essential emergency shelter for women fleeing abuse.

Assertion 2
 	
Evidence Pathos
 	
Evidence Ethos
 	
Evidence Logos
	II Many women and children are turned away from emergency shelters every day as a result of overcrowding and lack of alternate refuge.
	    A. Imagine you are a victim of domestic abuse. You finally find the courage to stop the hitting, kicking, screaming, biting and name-calling. You are taking your kids, some clothes and a few dollars to the emergency abuse shelter to begin the long road to recovery and a new life, only to find that the shelter is too full and you must return home or live life on the unpredictable, cold and equally violent streets.
	    B. In a "call to action" roundtable discussion Mayor Bart Peterson was quoted as saying that "in Indianapolis there are only two shelters where victims can go, the Julian Center and the Salvation Army. However, limited resources force the Julian Center and Salvation Army to turn away hundreds of victims each year." (Mayor)
	    C. In 2003, The National Coalition Against Domestic Violence Stated that in Indiana shelters were unable to house 1,471 domestic violence victims. (Indiana)

Evidence Logos	D. According to The Family Violence Prevention Fund website at www.endabuse.com, in 2000 nearly 296,000 women and children were not able to access essential emergency shelter for battered women. (The facts)
Evidence Logos	E. These are all upsetting facts particularly because there are three times as many animal shelters as abuse shelters in this country. (Trauma)
Restatement of Claim:	Therefore, I ask you to agree with me that domestic violence is a serious issue in this country and that there are insufficient alternatives for victims of domestic abuse.

Works Cited

Indiana Domestic Violence Statistics. *Indiana Coalition Against Domestic Violence.* June 2005. 12 Nov. 2005 <http://www.violenceresource.org/stats.htm>.

Indiana. Mayor Bart Peterson. Office of the Mayor. *Building a World Class City Neighborhood by Neighborhood.* 1 Sept. 1999. 12 Nov. 2005 <http://www.indygov.org/egov/mayor/plan/peterson_plan_1/part1.htm>.

The Facts on Housing and Domestic Violence. *Family Violence Prevention Fund.* 12 Nov. 2005 <http://endabuse.org>.

Trauma & recovery. The Julian Center. 9 Nov. 2005 <http://www.juliancenter.org/more_facts.html>.

Self-Evaluation
Reagan LaCour
Need Step Argument

My argument that there is an increasing need for support for victims of domestic violence is very solid. I have presented multiple statistics and examples to convince the audience that there is, in fact, a real problem with sufficient domestic violence resources. With these facts, I used a PowerPoint presentation to reinforce the startling numbers. The background showed a picture of a women looking downward, shamefully. This will appeal to the emotional listeners in the audience. I also used many credible resources. My sources are all recognized organizations against domestic violence and one source is from Indianapolis Mayor Bart Peterson. I cited exact addresses to confirm their validity and cited them orally as well.

I created stress within the audience with both my statistics about the classroom survey results and a story placing the audience in the victim's shoes. Both of these examples contribute to the audience feeling like they are part of the problem—not just outsiders looking in.

Overall, I was satisfied with my language and delivery. I felt that my passion for the subject was presented in a way that the audience would be able to really feel that I was speaking directly to them-and that I wanted their attention. My use of strong eye contact, gestures and strong voice and volume, all contributed to a powerful and persuasive speech.

Because the speech only required that we speak from our outline, I did feel that my speech lacked some extemporaneous style. I also felt like a louder inflection of my voice when I talk about the startling facts would have contributed to a better speech.

An area of my speech that could use further tweaking, was my use of persuasive language. I did not use passive language at all, so I could have been more convincing. I once had a teacher tell me I used too much flare in my writing, therefore I try to get to the point with clear, concise language.

However, I see how using words like "in dire need of your help" could be more convincing. I will certainly revaluate that area for my next speech. An example of where I could have used more persuasive language was in my introduction and conclusion. In my introduction, I simply stated my problem statement. I should have said that I am here to prove that domestic violence is a serious issue in our country and that battered women are not served adequately and are in dire need of our help.

My outline for speech #4 should satisfy the need step for speech #5. I feel that I have created an argument that will make the audience want to contribute to helping solve this problem. After the need step of my speech 5 the audience should understand that this is a serious problem and needs a solution. The numbers of domestic violence victims and the amount of victims being turned away are undeniable.

THE SPEECH TO PERSUADE ON A QUESTION OF POLICY

What Is a Speech on a Question of Policy and Why Is it Required?

Should your roommate take a basic speech course in his freshman year or wait? Should your parents buy a new computer now and risk being outdated in 6 months? Should you invest in bonds or mutual funds? Should the State of Indiana raise the driving age to 18? Should the federal government enact stricter gun control measures?

If you have dealt with or argued about any of these or similar issues, you have been in a situation involving a question of policy. This type of question deals with whether something should or should not be done and what specific course of action to take as a result. We have included it as a speech requirement because of our belief that your ability to influence the behavior of others is a critical life skill.

For this speech ask: What do you want your audience to *do* as a result of your speech? How do you want them to *behave*? What *action* do you want them to take? Do you want them to give blood? Start saving for retirement? Begin exercising? Petition their legislators? Specifically, whatever it is that you want them to do should be reflected in your specific purpose statement. How or why you want them to do it should be your central idea. Your goal is to change how your audience acts!

Your audience's responses, after hearing this speech, should include the following reactions:

- I am interested because this problem affects my life.

- I am mentally convinced that there is a serious problem; it is real and it affects my life because the evidence is sufficient, credible and logical.

- I feel like doing something because the evidence is so compelling or upsetting that I want to do something.

- I am motivated to act because the plan, as proposed, relieves the problem, is effective, beneficial, and easy for me to do.

- I will do it. Tell me how to do it.

The Monroe Motivated Sequence, which is the persuasive organizational pattern that you will use in this speech, leads the listener step-by-step to the desired action (your specific purpose.) There are unique audience responses for each step, which should be initiated by the speaker. For a complete break-down of the Monroe Sequence, audience responses to each step and the tasks of the speaker that are needed to create these responses, see section following speech requirements.

What Skills You Will Learn/Practice

1. You will learn to **formulate a specific purpose** and **central idea** on a question of policy with the intent toward immediate action.

2. You will **practice collecting audience data** which will assist you in constructing an argument.

3. You will continue to practice **discerning and researching evidence** from credible sources.

4. You will learn to organize your material according to *Monroe's Motivated Sequence.*

5. You will practice a **delivery style** in which your audience perceives your conviction/passion.

6. You will construct **an attention-getting, relevant introduction and a memorable conclusion.**

Examples of Questions of Policy (These are NOT Specific Purposes):

1. Should you have your taxes done professionally or should you do them yourself?

2. Should you begin a retirement plan while you are a student?

3. Should all people be required to volunteer for community/national service?

4. Should we ban all weapons of mass destruction?

5. Should all students be required to own a computer upon entering college?

What Are the Requirements for this Speech?

1. . . . appropriate topic and clearly-worded **specific purpose** and **central idea**

2. . . . an audience **survey** and **Audience Analysis/Adaptation Sheet**

3. . . . organization of material according to *Monroe's Motivated Sequence*

4. . . . a typed or word-processed **preparation outline** with the following functions labeled:

   ■ introduction and parts

   ■ body and parts

   ■ conclusion and parts

   ■ transitions, internal previews, internal summaries written out

- physical behaviors labeled in right-hand column
- assertions labeled
- evidence/proof types named and labeled

5. ... orally cite **5 different sources,** document in-text and on Works Cited page

6. ... one **audio-visual aid**—minimum

7. ... no more than **3 note cards**

8. ... speak **no less than 6 1/2 and no more than 7 1/2 minutes**

9. ... review your videotape and return the **Self-Evaluation** by instructor's deadline.

10. ... OTHER

Task Checklist (✔ Check off as you complete each one)

❏ 1. Choose a **subject** appropriate to the assignment.

❏ 2. Construct your **specific purpose.**

❏ 3. Create a **survey instrument** for your class and administer it. Collect data and make inferences and indicate adaptations on **Audience Analysis/Adaptation Sheet.**

❏ 4. **Research** your speech purpose.

❏ 5. **Choose evidence** based on inferences made from audience survey. Construct argument according to *Monroe's Motivated Sequence.*

❏ 6. Create your **preparation outline.**

❏ 7. Create your **audio-visual aid.** Save your visuals to RESOURCES in Oncourse CL. Bring visuals to class on a flash drive or CDROM.

❏ 8. **Practice** from preparation outline with instructional aid. Time. Edit. Time again.

❏ 9. Create **note cards.** *DO NOT write out your speech or preparation outline word-for-word on your note cards!* Practice. Time. Edit. Time.

❏ 10. Check room situation. Check your **appearance** (presentational image).

❏ 11. Hand your instructor your **preparation outline with Outline Grading Sheet attached, Audience Analysis/Adaptation Sheet** and **survey,** and both copies of the **Speaker Evaluation Sheet** before you speak.

❏ 12. **Review your videotape** after you have spoken. Thoughtfully write your **Self-Evaluation** and submit it to your instructor as required.

Grading Criteria

Grading Criteria for this Speech: See the Speaker Evaluation form and the Outline Grading Sheet in the Coursebook. *Apply these criteria to what you have prepared in order to optimize your grade points.*

Monroe's Motivated Sequence – Audience Response and Speaker Tasks

The following information is included to assist you in understanding the psychology and application of Monroe's Motivated Sequence. In each section below you will see two lists. The first list in each step details the necessary audience responses you must create in order to begin influencing your audience to act on your specific purpose. The second list includes necessary tasks that you must do in order to create these responses. Read them carefully.

Attention Step (interest)

Response speaker must create in audience:

- **This seems to be a problem;**
- **it is serious;**
- **it affects me and mine;**
- **I am interested.**

To create this response, the speaker must:

- **Call attention to problem.**
- **Reveal purpose/problem.**
- **Prepare audience/create relevance to audience.**
- **Reveal credibility of speaker.**
- **Preview purpose.**

Need Step (problem) (This is speech #4)

Response speaker must create in audience:

- **This IS a problem!**
- **It is exists, is serious, and affects me.**
- **I am upset, frustrated, infuriated.**
- **Something needs to be done about it.**

To create this response, the speaker must:

- **prove that a problem exists, is serious, and is affecting people directly or indirectly with well-reasoned evidence:**
  - **Logos — empirically verifiable, examples**
  - **Ethos — sources with substantial credibility**
  - **Pathos — stories or examples that appeal to the emotions such as personal testimony.**

Satisfaction Step (solution)

Response speaker must create in audience:

- Something CAN be done about this.
- It has been done successfully in other places.
- If this plan is effective, the problem will be gone or alleviated..
- I think I might want to help with the solution/plan.

To create this response, the speaker must:

- Describe a PLAN or solution to satisfy the problem or need. Be specific.
- Prove that it will work.
- Prove that it worked in other instances.
- Prove that it is possible/ doable. Use:

Kinds of support (EVIDENCE)

- Logos — empirically verifiable facts, examples, statistics.
- Ethos — sources with high credibility
- Pathos — support that appeals to the emotions

Visualization Step (benefit)

Response speaker must create in audience:

- If this plan is implemented, the problem might be solved!
- This plan has been beneficial in other circumstances.
- I would feel good about helping to solve this problem.
- Others will feel good.
- This will benefit everyone and things will be much better.

To create this response, the speaker must provide:

Kinds of support (EVIDENCE)

- Logos — empirically verifiable, examples, comparisons, case studies, etc.
- Ethos — sources with high credibility
- Pathos — support that appeals to the emotions, such as personal testimony, case histories, etc.

Action Step (resolution/response)

Response speaker must create in audience:

- I want to do this.

- This will make a difference.

- This is not so hard. I can do this.

- I will do this. Tell me how to do this.

To create this response, the speaker must:

- Describe action that audience needs to take.

- Make it feasible by stating specifically the process or procedure that listener needs to follow.

- Call for action.

- Appeal to audience sense of satisfaction with a memorable story or illustration.

PERSUASION POLICY SPEECH: AUDIENCE ANALYSIS/ADAPTATION

Directions:

Type or word-process the answers to these questions after you have conducted your survey. Use this information to guide the preparation of your speech.

NOTE: Attach a copy of your survey questionnaire with results summarized to this analysis.

---

1. What are you attempting to persuade your audience to **DO** as a result of your speech? (SP)

2. As a result of your questionnaire how many of your audience already follow this course of action? Why? How many do not? Why not? What does this suggest you must do?

3. According to your questionnaire, what objections do people have for NOT following your suggested action? What does this tell you about what must happen in the need and satisfaction steps?

4. According to your questionnaire, what are the significant beliefs or attitudes held by members of your audience that will affect their desire to follow the action you suggest? How will you handle this in your speech?

5. Based on the answers above, how can you motivate your audience toward your specific purpose? How will you effectively call them to action?

6. List each of your sources and explain why you chose them and how you will use each in your speech.

ASSIGNMENT #7

Policy Speech—Persuasive

Speaker Evaluation Sheet

I visited the Speaker's Lab for this assignment. Circle one.   YES   NO

Name _____   Section _____   Date _____

Specific Purpose and Central Idea (SP/CI) _____

	Points/Score	Comments
ATTENTION STEP (Introduction)		
▓ Gained attention/interest	____/____	
▓ Revealed policy topic clearly (SP)	____/____	
▓ Showed relevance to audience	____/____	
▓ Established speaker credibility	____/____	
▓ Articulated clear preview of speech	____/____	
NEED STEP (Body)		
▓ Clearly described need /problem	____/____	
▓ Used strong evidence showing need/ problem severity	____/____	
▓ Used strong evidence showing need/ problem affects audience	____/____	
SATISFACTION STEP (Body)		
▓ Described clear, workable solution/satisfaction plan	____/____	
▓ Used effective evidence to support plan	____/____	
VISUALIZATION STEP (Body)		
▓ Explained relevant benefits	____/____	
▓ Provided effective evidence of benefit.	____/____	
ACTION STEP (Conclusion)		
▓ Prepared audience for ending	____/____	
▓ Clearly explained specific actions.	____/____	
▓ Closed with specific/powerful call to action	____/____	
▓ Final appeal	____/____	
Delivery		
▓ Used extemporaneous style	____/____	
▓ Maintained consistent eye contact	____/____	
▓ Used voice and body effectively throughout speech	____/____	
▓ Used note cards effectively	____/____	
▓ Showed evidence of preparation and practice	____/____	
▓ Showed evidence of personal passion, involvement	____/____	
Overall		
▓ Maintained time parameters	____/____	
▓ Selected, prepared and used visual aids effectively	____/____	
▓ Used clear and convincing language	____/____	
▓ Used minimum of 5 credible sources, effectively cited	____/____	
▓ Used effective transitions between points	____/____	
* SPEECH SCORE	____/____	

ASSIGNMENT #7

Policy Speech—Persuasive

Speaker Evaluation Sheet

I visited the Speaker's Lab for this assignment. Circle one.   **YES   NO**

Name _____ Section _____ Date _____

Specific Purpose and Central Idea (SP/CI) _____

	Points/Score	Comments

ATTENTION STEP (Introduction)
- Gained attention/interest _____/_____
- Revealed policy topic clearly (SP) _____/_____
- Showed relevance to audience _____/_____
- Established speaker credibility _____/_____
- Articulated clear preview of speech _____/_____

NEED STEP (Body)
- Clearly described need /problem _____/_____
- Used strong evidence showing need/ problem severity _____/_____
- Used strong evidence showing need/ problem affects audience _____/_____

SATISFACTION STEP (Body)
- Described clear, workable solution/satisfaction plan _____/_____
- Used effective evidence to support plan _____/_____

VISUALIZATION STEP (Body)
- Explained relevant benefits _____/_____
- Provided effective evidence of benefit. _____/_____

ACTION STEP (Conclusion)
- Prepared audience for ending _____/_____
- Clearly explained specific actions. _____/_____
- Closed with specific/powerful call to action _____/_____
- Final appeal _____/_____

Delivery
- Used extemporaneous style _____/_____
- Maintained consistent eye contact _____/_____
- Used voice and body effectively throughout speech _____/_____
- Used note cards effectively _____/_____
- Showed evidence of preparation and practice _____/_____
- Showed evidence of personal passion, involvement _____/_____

Overall
- Maintained time parameters _____/_____
- Selected, prepared and used visual aids effectively _____/_____
- Used clear and convincing language _____/_____
- Used minimum of 5 credible sources, effectively cited _____/_____
- Used effective transitions between points _____/_____

* SPEECH SCORE _____/_____

ASSIGNMENT #7

Policy Speech—Persuasive

ATTACH THIS SHEET TO YOUR OUTLINE

Name _____ Section _____ Date _____

Criteria for grading your outline are as follows: Points/Score

Topic/Format

■ Wrote clear, narrow SP and CI   _____
■ Used 3-column outline, neat   _____
■ Proper coordination, subordination, symbolization, indentation _____
■ Labeled types of reasoning used   _____
■ Labeled types of proof used   _____
■ Wrote assertions and support in complete, declarative sentences _____

Attention Step—labeled (introduction)

■ Crafted and labeled all 5 parts of introduction   _____

Need, Satisfaction, Visualization Steps—labeled (body)

■ Developed fully and labeled Need, Satisfaction, Visualization Steps _____
■ Transitions written out and labeled   _____
■ Cited all sources in-text of outline with parenthetical notation _____
■ One idea/fact per symbol

Action Step-labeled (conclusion)

■ Created and labled 3-part action step   _____
■ Labeled Call to Action   _____

Over-all

■ Note cards reflect preparation outline   _____
■ Cited 5 sources (minimum) on Works Cited page (MLA)   _____
■ OTHER _____   _____
■ OTHER _____   _____

TOTAL OUTLINE SCORE   _____

PERSUASION POLICY SPEECH: PEER LISTENING SHEET (1)

Speaker _____   Listener _____

Topic _____

A. Organization

Write one sentence describing each step in the speaker's argument or a concern and a suggestion for improvement if necessary.

1. Attention—How did the speaker get my attention?

2. Need—What is the need to be satisfied? (What is the problem?)

3. Satisfaction—What is the plan?

4. Visualization—How will it benefit me?

5. Action—What do I have to do? Is the plan feasible for me?

B. Delivery

Give examples of convincing language exhibited by the speaker.

C. Personal Response (Check one)

❑ I am moved to act and here's why . . .

❑ I still need more information such as . . .

❑ I remain neutral and here's why . . .

❑ I am now willing to reconsider my position and here's why . . .

❑ I am not moved to act and here's why . . .

PERSUASION POLICY SPEECH:
PEER LISTENING SHEET (2)

Speaker _____   Listener _____

Topic _____

A. Organization

Write one sentence describing each step in the speaker's argument or a concern and a suggestion for improvement if necessary.

1. Attention—How did the speaker get my attention?

2. Need—What is the need to be satisfied? (What is the problem?)

3. Satisfaction—What is the plan?

4. Visualization—How will it benefit me?

5. Action—What do I have to do? Is the plan feasible for me?

B. Delivery

Give examples of convincing language exhibited by the speaker.

C. Personal Response (Check one)

❏ I am moved to act and here's why . . .

❏ I still need more information such as . . .

❏ I remain neutral and here's why . . .

❏ I am now willing to reconsider my position and here's why . . .

❏ I am not moved to act and here's why . . .

PERSUASION POLICY SPEECH: PEER LISTENING SHEET (3)

Speaker _____ Listener _____

Topic _____

A. Organization

Write one sentence describing each step in the speaker's argument or a concern and a suggestion for improvement if necessary.

1. Attention—How did the speaker get my attention?

2. Need—What is the need to be satisfied? (What is the problem?)

3. Satisfaction—What is the plan?

4. Visualization—How will it benefit me?

5. Action—What do I have to do? Is the plan feasible for me?

B. Delivery

Give examples of convincing language exhibited by the speaker.

C. Personal Response (Check one)

❏ I am moved to act and here's why . . .

❏ I still need more information such as . . .

❏ I remain neutral and here's why . . .

❏ I am now willing to reconsider my position and here's why . . .

❏ I am not moved to act and here's why . . .

PERSUASION POLICY SPEECH:
PEER LISTENING SHEET (4)

Speaker _____   Listener _____

Topic _____

A. Organization

Write one sentence describing each step in the speaker's argument or a concern and a suggestion for improvement if necessary.

1. Attention—How did the speaker get my attention?

2. Need—What is the need to be satisfied? (What is the problem?)

3. Satisfaction—What is the plan?

4. Visualization—How will it benefit me?

5. Action—What do I have to do? Is the plan feasible for me?

B. Delivery

Give examples of convincing language exhibited by the speaker.

C. Personal Response (Check one)

❏ I am moved to act and here's why . . .

❏ I still need more information such as . . .

❏ I remain neutral and here's why . . .

❏ I am now willing to reconsider my position and here's why . . .

❏ I am not moved to act and here's why . . .

PERSUASION POLICY SPEECH: PEER LISTENING SHEET (5)

Speaker _____   Listener _____

Topic _____

A. Organization

Write one sentence describing each step in the speaker's argument or a concern and a suggestion for improvement if necessary.

1. Attention—How did the speaker get my attention?

2. Need—What is the need to be satisfied? (What is the problem?)

3. Satisfaction—What is the plan?

4. Visualization—How will it benefit me?

5. Action—What do I have to do? Is the plan feasible for me?

B. Delivery

Give examples of convincing language exhibited by the speaker.

C. Personal Response (Check one)

❑ I am moved to act and here's why . . .

❑ I still need more information such as . . .

❑ I remain neutral and here's why . . .

❑ I am now willing to reconsider my position and here's why . . .

❑ I am not moved to act and here's why . . .

PERSUASION POLICY SPEECH: PEER LISTENING SHEET (6)

Speaker _____ Listener _____

Topic _____

A. Organization

Write one sentence describing each step in the speaker's argument or a concern and a suggestion for improvement if necessary.

1. Attention—How did the speaker get my attention?

2. Need—What is the need to be satisfied? (What is the problem?)

3. Satisfaction—What is the plan?

4. Visualization—How will it benefit me?

5. Action—What do I have to do? Is the plan feasible for me?

B. Delivery

Give examples of convincing language exhibited by the speaker.

C. Personal Response (Check one)

❏ I am moved to act and here's why . . .

❏ I still need more information such as . . .

❏ I remain neutral and here's why . . .

❏ I am now willing to reconsider my position and here's why . . .

❏ I am not moved to act and here's why . . .

PERSUASION POLICY SPEECH: PEER LISTENING SHEET (7)

Speaker _____   Listener _____

Topic _____

A. Organization

Write one sentence describing each step in the speaker's argument or a concern and a suggestion for improvement if necessary.

1. Attention—How did the speaker get my attention?

2. Need—What is the need to be satisfied? (What is the problem?)

3. Satisfaction—What is the plan?

4. Visualization—How will it benefit me?

5. Action—What do I have to do? Is the plan feasible for me?

B. Delivery

Give examples of convincing language exhibited by the speaker.

C. Personal Response (Check one)

❏ I am moved to act and here's why . . .

❏ I still need more information such as . . .

❏ I remain neutral and here's why . . .

❏ I am now willing to reconsider my position and here's why . . .

❏ I am not moved to act and here's why . . .

Persuasion Policy Speech: Self-Evaluation Sheet

Directions

Review your speech from your video tape. Write a **reflective narrative** evaluating your performance based on the questions below. Be sure your work is typed or word-processed. See sample self-evaluation in the section following.

- Did I spend enough time gathering information/preparing/practicing? Explain.

- Did I choose strong ethical support? Give examples.

- Were the parts of the Monroe Motivated Sequence well-developed? Why or why not?

- Is it likely the audience could effectively repeat my argument themselves after seeing my speech?

- Was my delivery appropriate (eye contact, body language, passionate attitude, articulation, enthusiasm)?

- Did I achieve the time limits? Why or why not?

- How did I use my note cards? Be specific.

- I did the following things effectively:

- I need to work on the following:

- How have I improved overall in the art of public speaking?

The Speech to Persuade on a Question of Policy

These documents are examples of student work. They are included to give you an idea of how to prepare your speech materials and the quality of work expected. All student work is printed with student permission and is subject to U.S. copyright law.

S
A
M
P
L
E

REAGAN LACOUR
First Place Winner,
Speech Night
FALL 2005

Survey Results for Policy Speech
Reagan LaCour
Section 2651
13 students responded

Have you been a victim of domestic violence?
9-no, 4-yes

How about your parents? Family? Friends?
4-no, 9-yes

If you were a victim, where did you turn to for help?
9-n/a, 1-no where, 3-friends & family

If someone else, where did they go?
4-n/a, 3-friends & family, 3-divorce, 1-police, 1-army, 1-no where

Have you ever volunteered at abuse shelters? Why or why not?
11-no, 2-yes
Why?-for school, likes to volunteer
Why not?-never considered it, not well enough informed

Have you ever donated money to abuse shelters? Why or why not?
8-no, 5-yes
Why not? - never considered, not well enough informed, not enough money

If not-what would make you more inclined to do so?
1-no response, 4-n/a, 7-more info, 1-if knew someone personally

If you have-what would make you do so again?
1-more time, 1-knowing benefit shelter, 1-its the right thing to do, 1-thought of what would happen otherwise

Audience Analysis/Policy Speech
Reagan LaCour
Section 2651

1. **What are you attempting to persuade your audience to DO as a result of your speech?**

As a result of this speech, I am attempting to persuade the audience to donate time or money to battered women's shelters.

2. **How many of your audience already follow this course of action? Why? How many do not? Why not? What does this suggest you must do in the attention step?**

Of the 13 students that responded to the survey, only 2 have volunteered at a shelter and only 5 have donated money to a shelter.

3. **What objections do people have for NOT following your suggested action? What does this tell you about what must happen in the need and satisfaction steps?**

None of the students surveyed were against my suggested action. However, many students were uniformed about domestic abuse shelters and felt that they would be more inclined to donate time or money to a shelter if they had more information about them. Secondly, with this lack of knowledge, students are obviously not aware of the importance of these shelters or how in need they are of support.

4. **Who, then, is your target audience? Can you expand your target audience? How?**

Because many of the students were victims of domestic violence or close to a victim, they are the immediate target audience because of their interest. However, I can expand my target audience by proving how prevalent domestic violence is in the United States and how vulnerable we all are to this problem.

5. **Are there any significant beliefs or attitudes held by your audience which will affect their desire to follow the action you suggest? How does this affect your visualization step?**

Unlike some other persuasion speech topics, mine is not one that people argue its importance. The biggest hurdle is to inform people of exactly how these shelters work, what they to do make a real difference in the lives of victims and how even a small contribution can make a big difference in the lives of the victims.

6. **Based on the answers above, how can you motivate your audience toward your specific purpose? (How will you effectively call them to action?)**

The most effective way for me to motivate my audience to donate time or money to these shelters is to inform them about the shelters, explain the needs of the shelters, eliminate the audiences' concerns about their ability to contribute and show them how easy it is to help. It is also very important that the audience be emotionally drawn to the topic. Using real-life experience and startling statistics, I intend for the audience to be feel the need to want to help.

Persuasion Policy Speech Outline

Reagan LaCour
R110—2651
November 28, 2005

Title: *Take a stand, make a change.*

Specific Purpose: To persuade my audience to donate time or money to local women and children domestic abuse shelters.

Central Problem Statement: Due to the prevalence of domestic violence, there is a need to increase support for resources and assistance for its victims.

	INTRODUCTION	
Attention Step (Pathos)	I. I remember that day as is if it were yesterday. My two older brothers, Rick and Rodney, and I stood in the entryway of our home, watching in terror, as our dad threw plates, silverware and glasses at our mom. My oldest brother Rick took Rodney and me into his room while our dad beat our mom so badly that to this day-she can still only turn her head so far one way. The next day my mom took shelter with a coworker, while the police put my brothers and me in short-term foster care. My mom later said that if she ever returned home during another fit of anger—he would have killed her. I was three years old and this is the only memory I have of my parent's marriage. My mom was blessed with the strength to leave and the opportunity to take shelter with a friend. Not every domestic violence victim has that choice. Many victims stay in abusive relationships because they have no where to go.	Eye Contact!
Reveal Topic	II. There are inadequate resources and assistance for victims of domestic violence.	
Relevancy (Logos)	III. The Surgeon General recently declared domestic violence the number one health issue facing the United States today. Of the 13 students that responded to my R110 class survey, 9 were either victims of domestic abuse or were close to a victim, this was a startling 70%. (Trauma)	
Credibility	IV I have had personal experience with domestic violence and I have made it my goal to research the seriousness of domestic violence in this country and the resources we provide to victims.	
Preview	V. Today, I will confirm the prevalence of domestic violence in this country, prove we lack assistance for abuse victims, encourage you to donate time or money to battered women's shelters, and prove how this will benefit victims of domestic violence.	

	BODY	
Need Step (Claim)	**I. There are insufficient resources for victims.**	
Assertion	A. Domestic violence is one of the most prevalent issues facing women in the United States today.	
Evidence (Logos)	1. A women is beaten every nine seconds in the United States. (Trauma)	Begin Power-Point
Evidence (Logos)	2. According to a recent study, domestic violence is the primary cause of injury to women between the ages of 15 and 44—more than auto accidents, muggings and rapes combined. (Trauma)	Next slide
Evidence (Logos)	3. The Indiana Coalition Against Domestic Violence stated that in Marion County, more than 20,000 women are victims of domestic abuse each year. (Indiana)	Next slide

Next slide (goes to black) |
Evidence (Ethos)	4. Domestic abuse holds no ethnic or socioeconomic prejudice. It affects people of all cultures and economic class. Many prominent figures have been victims of domestic abuse such as: Christina Aguilera, Christina Applegate, Brett Butler (a famous comedian), Oprah Winfrey and Tina Turner, to name a few.	Next slide
Transition	Now that I have confirmed the prevalence of domestic violence in the United States, let me prove that there is a lack of essential emergency shelter for women fleeing abuse.	Next slide (goes to black)
Assertion	B. Many women and children are turned away from emergency shelters every day as a result of overcrowding and lack of alternate refuge.	
Evidence (Ethos)	1. In a "call to action" roundtable discussion Mayor Bart Peterson was quoted as saying that "in Indianapolis there are only two shelters where victims can go, The Julian Center and The Salvation Army. However, limited resources often force The Julian Center and Salvation Army to turn away hundreds of victims each year. (Mayor)	
Evidence (Ethos)	2. The Julian's Center 2004 Annual Report stated that the facility was at capacity, requiring families to sleep in the library and homework room. (The Julian)	Next slide
Evidence (Logos)	3. In 2003, The National Coalition Against Domestic Violence stated that in Indiana, shelters were unable to house 1,471 domestic violence victims. (Indiana)	Next slide

Evidence (Logos)	4. According to The Family Violence Prevention Fund website, in 2000 nearly 296,000 women and children were not able to access essential emergency shelter for battered women. (The facts)	Next slide
Evidence (Logos)	5. These are all upsetting facts particularly because there are three times as many animal shelters as abuse shelters in this country. (Trauma)	Next slide
Transition	Now that you know how serious the problem of insufficient assistance for domestic violence is in the United States and in Indiana, let me explain how we can improve the available resources for victims.	Next slide (goes to black)
Satisfaction Step	**II. Donating time and money or resources will directly benefit these shelters and the victims they serve.** A. Choosing to donate money to facilities such as The Julian Center is both very beneficial and easy to do.	
Evidence (Logos)	1. The 2004 Annual Julian Center report stated that public donations account for 47.2% of their funding. (The Julian) 2. You can sponsor a family of your choice, donate to specific programs of the shelter, or make a blind donation to the shelter to go towards whatever they choose.	Next slide
	3. At the end of my presentation I will be handing out Julian Center brochures with their phone number listings as well as donation forms. B. If you are a struggling student, like the majority of us, and you cannot afford a monetary donation you may also donate clothing and goods.	Next slide (goes to black)
	1. Donating items from The Julian Centers "wish list" is also beneficial to the shelter. The less money the organization spends on these items the more they can devote to the actual housing of the victims. 2. These items vary from household goods to clothing.	Next slide
	C. You can also choose to do volunteer work. 1. Volunteering for the shelter can take as little or as much time as you like. Some work is as an on-need basis and some is weekly or monthly.	Next slide

	2. The Julian Center has several opportunities for volunteers, from working the child care center to helping at special events.	
Transition	Now that you know how easy it is to help these abuse victims, let's take a look at how your donations can make a difference.	Next slide (goes to black)
Visualization Step Evidence (Logos)	**III. There are so many benefits to your donations and volunteer work.** A. $10 will provide emergency transportation to The Julian Center for a woman and her children fleeing their abuser. As little as $18 will feed a mother and two children breakfast, lunch and dinner; and $60 will house a family for an emergency night stay. (The Julian) 1. Imagine the joy you would bring to a mother and child with just a few dollars. 2. With as little as $20 dollars a month you could house four different families in a year. B. If you choose to volunteer instead of donate, you could save the shelter hundreds of thousands of dollars in wages and salaries which account for the majority of the center's operating expenses. (The Julian)	Next slide Next slide (goes to black)
Restate Claim *Action Step*	**CONCLUSION** I. Therefore, I would like to reiterate how you can make a difference in a domestic violence victim's life. I want to encourage you all to take action against this continuous problem for so many innocent and helpless women and children. I ask that each of you take home a donation form and give whatever amount you can afford. It is our duty to ensure the comfort and safety of these victims. There are some important things to know for when you decide to make your contribution. A. Donating money to the Julian Center is as easy as filling out a form with your donation information such as your name and address, amount and type of payment, as well as anyone the donation may be honoring. B. You may also pay over-the-phone if you are using a credit card. C. Ifyou go to the center's website you can always find an updated list of current needs from their "wish list", and you can take these items to their 'Thrifty Threads' donation hub located at 86th street and Ditch Road.	 Next slide Next slide

	D. As a volunteer, there is an initial orientation meeting from 6:00 to 8:00 p.m. on the 1st Tuesday of each month. You can feel free to contact the Julian Center with regards to these opportunities.	Next slide
	E. I will be handing out Julian Center informational packets at the end of my presentation which will answer address and phone number questions.	Next slide (goes to black)
Review Main Points	II. Today, I have undoubtedly confirmed the prevalence of domestic violence in this country, proved we lack proper resources for these victims, explained how we can help this cause, and where our assistance will benefit victims.	
Clincher	III. When I was three years old I was not able to help my mom. Fortunately, others were. Now I am able to help so many others in our situation, and so are you. Do Not let others fall victim to the vicious cycle of abuse with no where to turn. Take A Stand, Make A Change, Make A Donation!	

Works Cited

Indiana Domestic Violence Statistics. *Indiana Coalition Against Domestic Violence.* June 2005. 12 Nov. 2005 <http://www.violenceresource.org/stats.htm>.

Indiana. Mayor Bart Peterson. Office of the Mayor. *Building a World Class City Neighborhood by Neighborhood.* 1 Sept. 1999. 12 Nov. 2005 <http://www.indygov.org/egov/mayor/plan/peterson_plan_1/part1.htm>.

The Facts on Housing and Domestic Violence. *Family Violence Prevention Fund.* 12 Nov. 2005 <http://endabuse.org>.

The Julian Center 2004 Annual Report. Indianapolis: The Julian Center, 2004.

Trauma & recovery. The Julian Center. 9 Nov. 2005 <http://www.juliancenter.org/more_facts.html>.

Self-Evaluation: Persuasion Policy Speech
Reagan LaCour

Overall, I am very satisfied with the results of my final speech. Because I was able to relate to the topic through personal experience, I found myself being more passionate about finding important and relevant information. The majority of my time spent preparing for the speech was during the research step. I researched various books, articles and domestic violence websites to ensure that I gathered plenty of evidence to support my argument. Once I had an abundance of information, I took a lot of time to organize the information into sections that allowed the information to have a clear and steady flow. My next step was to prepare my outline following Monroe's Motivated Sequence. I prepared the outline initially, and then adjusted and readjusted the information so that the audience would be able to follow the speech while feeling an impact from the topic.

All of the examples I used in my speech were factual, astonishing, serious and emotional. It was very important that my audience understand both the seriousness of domestic violence in the United States and how victims are affected by the lack of resources and assistance when fleeing abuse. I began my speech with a personal story about my childhood and my mom's experience with domestic violence at the hands of my dad. It was important for me to include this story because it reassured the audience of my credibility with the topic, while gaining their attention. The other examples included statistical information such as how many women are beaten in Indiana and the United States and how insufficient funding and overcrowding affect shelters. In addition to the facts that were presented throughout my speech, I included a PowerPoint that helped the audience to visualize these relevant statistics. The combinations of written and visual communication make it very likely that the audience absorbed most of the information and could effectively repeat my argument in the future.

However, I believe that my speech was most persuasive and effective due to my attention to following Monroe's Motivated Sequence. Each part of the sequence was well-developed and thoroughly supported using both ethos and pathos. By following Monroe's sequence so closely, the audience feels a natural progression of the mind to recognize a need and want to make a change. Using this pattern, a speaker has the ability to persuade an audience, even if their delivery is not extremely powerful.

From my previous speeches, I found that over-preparation can lead to memorization. When a speech is memorized, there is a sense of humanity that can be lost. Because my topic addresses such serious issues, both personally and universally, it was very important that my sincerity be reflected. Therefore, when practicing this speech, I made sure that I did not over-practice or memorize, and I consciously remained aware of the emotional aspect of the speech.

Other functions of my speech, such as remaining within the time limits and proper use of my note cards were met with practice and preparation. Several "wordy" areas of my speech were eliminated to stay within the time limits. While it seemed frustrating at times, I realized afterwards that those words were not necessary to the function of the speech. When I prepared my note cards, I made sure to have short, simple sentences so that I only used them as reminders and mental post-its of my place in the speech. This method of preparing the note cards helped to ensure an extemporaneous delivery style.

The area of the speech that I was least satisfied with was my delivery. I gave the speech in a small classroom setting the previous week and I was unable to adjust my delivery style to the larger venue. I was able to maintain eye contact and strong body language, but I could have displayed a more passionate attitude with voice inflection and enthusiasm. While the speech addressed a topic that is naturally very somber, it would not have been inappropriate to be slightly more intense. Quite honestly, I became overwhelmed by my nerves. I had never been on a stage before and felt very small when I was speaking.

I did the following things well:

- Topic

- Organization

- Preparation

- Research

- Introduction and conclusion

- Following Monroe's Motivated Sequence

- Relating to the audience

- Credibility

- Remaining within time limits

- Proper use of note cards

- Proper use of PowerPoint

I need to work on the following:
- Adjusting delivery style to venue

- Allowing nerves to work for me rather than against me

- Maintaining strong visual presence

- Maintaining strong voice inflection

- Enthusiasm

Overall, I have improved greatly in the art of public speaking. While I have always been outgoing and find it easy to talk to people, I remained very unsure about my abilities in public speaking. After the completion of this course and the various speeches we were required to give, I found that I can be a very talented speaker and speech writer. I became more comfortable about speaking in front of an audience (although I have not perfected that skill), delivering a speech using extemporaneous style and preparing a well-written speech. I found that the key to being a proficient speaker is to choose topics that are interesting and prevalent to the audience, taking the time to do extensive and powerful research, organizing an effective speech and practicing.

APPENDIX 1

OUTSIDE SPEAKER REPORT—DIRECTIONS

Why Outside Speaker Reports Are Required

You have been busy giving speeches this semester and you have been "learning by doing." Getting up on your feet and putting into action what you have been studying has helped you improve your speaking skills. But in addition to doing, there is much to be gained by observing speakers outside of class and evaluating their speaking abilities. With this assignment you can forego the jitters and sit back and relax. You will listen with a critical ear and a watchful eye. You become "critic for the day."

While observing your speaker you will be evaluating this presentation using the same guidelines that your instructor has emphasized all semester. Do you think the speaker analyzed the audience when considering the topic and situation? Was the speech organized in such a way that the audience could follow and remember? Did the speaker employ effective delivery skills? What about research? You will never hear another speaker again without considering the essentials you have learned in R110.

Outside Speaker Report

This assignment requires that you go "outside" of the classroom to observe a speaker in action. This means that speeches by other classmates are not allowed, nor are homilies/sermons delivered by your pastors nor lectures delivered by other instructors.

You may choose either an informative or persuasive setting. The school newspaper is an excellent source for on-campus speakers. Many faculty groups, clubs and organizations bring in speakers to talk on a variety of topics. Pick something you are interested in or that relates to your major. Or you may take a different approach and deliberately go to see a speaker on a topic that you know nothing about. That would be the real test. Can the speaker get your interest and keep it? The Indianapolis newspaper also offers opportunities, primarily in the Thursday edition that highlights weekend activities. School bulletin boards also promote different offerings.

Once you have observed your speaker, use the following guidelines to write your report. Check your syllabus for the assigned due date.

OUTSIDE SPEAKER REPORT #1A– INFORMATIVE

A. **Identification—Make sure that the following information is included on the top of your paper.**

1. Your name

2. Instructor's name

3. Section number

4. Name of speaker observed/date and time of event

5. Today's date

B. **Observations—in a concise manner provide the following information:**

1. What was the speaker's desired response?

2. What is the physical setting from the speech? (How was the audience seated, where was the speaker relative to the audience, in what kind of facility and atmosphere was the speech presented?) (Chapter 5, Lucas)

3. What was the occasion for this speech?

4. What was the make-up of the audience?

   a. size

   b. ages

   c. sex

   d. race

   e. educational backgrounds

   f. knowledge about the topic

   g. relevant beliefs

   h. relevant attitudes

5. Could you easily identify the main points of the speech? What were they?

6. Was the introduction effective? Did it get your attention? Did it reveal the topic? Did the speaker establish his credibility? Did the preview occur? (Chapter 9, Lucas)

7. Was the conclusion effective? Did the speaker use circular construction? Did you hear the speaker signal the end? Were you left with a reinforcement of the central idea? (Chapter 9, Lucas)

8. What types of support were used? (Chapter 7, Lucas)

9. What types of connectives were used? Transitions, internal previews, internal summaries, signposts (Chapter 8, Lucas)?

10. Did the speaker employ credible sources?

11. Visual Delivery—Discuss volume, pitch, rate, pauses, vocal variety, pronunciation, articulation, and language choice.

12. Non-verbal communication—Include your observations about personal appearance, body actions, gestures, and eye contact.

C. What does this mean for me?

Explain your overall reaction to the speech. This is your opportunity to express your thoughts on the speaker's strengths and weaknesses. What two speaking techniques did you see used that you would want to use in **your** next speech? What would you tell this speaker to work on to improve his/her next speech?

OUTSIDE SPEAKER REPORT #1B– PERSUASIVE

Follow the same format for the informative outside speaker report, but add the following questions in section B of your report:

1. What type of organization did the speaker use? (For example, *Monroe Motivated Sequence* Chapter 15, Lucas)

2. Discuss the speaker's credibility. Did it change during the course of the speech? (initial/derived/terminal—Chapter 16, Lucas)

3. How well did the speaker use evidence? (Logic)

4. Did the speaker reason well, given the evidence employed? Did the speaker use any faulty reasoning (fallacies)?

5. What types of emotional appeals were used?

6. Were you persuaded? Why or why not?

Criteria for Grading

1. Your report should be thorough. Use the list of questions as a checklist.

2. Your report will be typed or word-processed. (No exceptions)

3. College level writing is expected.

Other Requirements/Comments From Your Instructor

_____

_____

_____

_____

_____

OUTSIDE SPEAKER REPORT #2

Your instructor may give you another option for your outside speaker report. This version asks you to analyze Martin Luther King's speech, "I Have A Dream." You can find the complete manuscript in the appendix of your textbook. This speech is also on the CD-ROM that comes with your textbook.

You may view this speech at the IUPUI University Library by accessing Martin Luther King, "I Have A Dream" via the IUCAT, Advanced Settings. Get the video off the shelf and view it using the facilities in the basement of the Library. At IUPUC, ask for the videotape at the reference desk.

After you have looked at the video and reviewed the manuscript, answer the following questions:

1. Summarize the occasion or setting for the speech. Include an identification of the date, the place and the audience. (You will need to do some research for this section.)

2. The speech has a specific organizational pattern. Identify the pattern and support your choice through references to the speech. (See Lucas Chapter 15)

3. Identify the three parts of the speech. Justify your choices.

4. Identify the stylistic/language devices used by King.

5. Comment on the impact the speech had on the audience and nation, then and now. You will need to do some research for this question.

Criteria for Grading

1. Your report should be thorough. Use the list of questions as a checklist.

2. Your report must be typed or word-processed. (No exceptions)

3. College level writing is expected.

Other Requirement/Comments From Your Instructor

_____

_____

_____

APPENDIX 2

Comparing and Contrasting Websites

COMPARING AND CONTRASTING WEBSITES

An In-Class Group Exercise

Today, anyone with something to say and a little technical know-how can publish on the World Wide Web. Scientists, educators, and scholars can report the results of their research quickly and easily, often well before a traditional journal might disseminate such data. Similarly, school-age youngsters with an Internet connection can develop a web site containing science fair experiment results that suggest a cause-effect relationship between El Niño and corporate profits! Take a critical look at each web site before you use it. A few minutes of careful, systematic analysis can save you hours of precious time, extreme embarrassment, or worse, a failing grade.

With your group or individually, compare and contrast two web sites along each of the dimensions shown. Jot your opinions in the corresponding boxes. Then decide which site would be more appropriate to use as a resource in a college-level research paper, and why.

	Web Site #1: http://www.martinlutherking.org	Web Site #2: http://www.thekingcenter.org
Author: Who is it? Credentials? Occupation? Position? Experience? Institutional affiliation? Can you tell?		
Purpose: What is the purpose for creating the site?		
Bias: Does the information seem slanted or biased? How?		
Information Source: How were data collected? Were sound research used? Are sources cited?		
Conclusions: What conclusions did the author reach? Are conclusions in line with the data presented?		
Relationship to other works: Compared to similar works, is site in tune with/in opposition to conventional wisdom?		
Attachments: Do charts, maps, bibliographies, etc., convey or detract from meaning?		
Currency: Is the site dated? When was it last updated?		
Mechanics: Does site contain helpful, working links to other sites? Links back to the main page?		
Organization: Is identifying information easy to find? Graphics consistent? Is there a "site map"?		

Prepared by Susan Schlag, IUPUI University Library, 8/98, from 'Evaluating Sources of Information on the Web, by Sharon Hay, 8/96.